SETBACKS *to* SUMMITS

Navigating Minds at Work from Setbacks to Summits in the New Digital Age

Roopa Raj

INDIA • SINGAPORE • MALAYSIA

ISBN 979-8-89067-858-4

Table of Contents

Acknowledgments

I extend my heartfelt gratitude to:

- My mother, an unwavering pillar of support throughout my life.
- My husband, a constant source of inspiration and an ardent advocate of my career, whom I look up to and learn from all the time.
- My children, who have stood by me like steadfast friends, demonstrating understanding, flexibility, and encouragement towards my work commitments. They are my lifelines!

I am also deeply thankful to the many friends who generously contributed their time to proofread and offer invaluable suggestions. Without their support, this book would not have progressed from the initial stages to completion. Your collective efforts have made this journey possible and profoundly meaningful.

Introduction

In the current era of the 21st century, digital technologies are profoundly reshaping our workplaces, far exceeding the expectations we held just a decade prior. While we have inundated ourselves with books, articles, and discussions on adapting to this dynamic digital environment, a crucial aspect often remains in the shadows: **the human psyche**—the real intellectual property at the core of all advancements.

As we further intertwine our lives with technology, it's imperative to address not just its future but also its convergence with the future of mental health. The potential lies not merely in understanding how technology is evolving but also in harnessing its evolution to address contemporary mental health challenges effectively.

Through my years spearheading digital transformations across the globe, I've marveled at the innovation, productivity, and business growth they catalyze. Simultaneously, I've witnessed the strain it places on individuals: the impending stress, the all-encompassing uncertainty, and the daunting feeling of being overwhelmed. These mental health challenges, if left unchecked, can ripple through teams, jeopardizing the overall efficacy of transformation initiatives. And with time, these challenges only seem to amplify.

Setbacks to Summits is a synthesis of these insights. This work not only amplifies the conversation around technology but anchors it with a spotlight on mental well-being. It recognizes that our cognitive faculties, mirroring the technological tools we employ, are crucial for achieving success in the workplace and thus deserve equal, if not more, attention and care.

Herein, you'll unearth practical insights derived from organizational behavior and technology management, punctuated with the genuine experiences of those in the throes of such metamorphoses. Whether you're an employee navigating changes in your role or recalibrating to a new role, a leader piloting your team through a digital shift, or an entrepreneur at the vanguard of innovation, the wisdom in these pages seeks to fortify your mental resilience, heighten awareness, and manage stress.

True success in this digital epoch isn't just about mastering technology but nurturing our mental well-being, supporting our colleagues, and valuing our cognitive assets. By centering our focus here, we unlock an avenue not only for enhanced mental wellness but also for heightened productivity and organizational growth. I envisage this book to be a compass, guiding you towards this holistic vision of success.

In penning this book, my primary aim has been to enlighten and assist the brilliant, dedicated, and inventive minds navigating the demands of the digital era. We discuss the importance of proactive mental health management for those blessed with acute cognitive abilities. Yet, while we strive to embrace the digital future with all the intellect at our disposal, there are children who, though no fault of their own, aren't privy to the full spectrum of mental capabilities. I believe that those of us fortunate enough to possess sharp minds bear a responsibility to support those who face cognitive challenges from the outset. It's with this thought that **I've decided to channel the proceeds from this book to charities dedicated to helping mentally underdeveloped children.** As you delve into the strategies and insights within these pages, know that you're not just investing in your well-being but also contributing to a brighter future for these children.

Let's navigate Minds at Work from ***Setbacks to Summits*** in the New Digital Age.

Chapter 1

Global Workplace Revolution: Opportunities Amidst Turmoil

On a recent visit to a San Francisco tech conference, I shared a cab with a seasoned tech executive and had an extremely thought-provoking conversation during the long commute. He unveiled the raw reality of his current ordeal: an arduous merger between his firm and another industry giant. While this was a fertile opportunity for growth, the journey had been taxing, testing everyone's resilience and agility. Employees were thrust into a sea of uncertainty and expected to keep their motivation afloat and demonstrate high levels of endurance and adaptability as the company continued to pursue building new products with emerging technologies and complete significant business transformations during the long merger process. This exchange cast a stark light on the human struggles simmering beneath the surface of our rapidly changing workplaces.

We continued to discuss how the modern professional world is more abundant with opportunities for professionals than ever before. Yet, it is this very richness and ceaseless evolution that creates a relentless demand for adaptation. The landscape is one where everyone appears to be coping, yet beneath the facade, many are staggering under the weight of change. Anxiety, mental stress, and worries about the future are more prevalent than we'd like to admit, often hidden under the pretense that ***it will pass.***

Given our leaps in technology, especially with AI, both of us began thinking of remediation and explored the possibility of an AI-powered tool that could intuitively understand and respond to our employees' distress signals. A tool that could offer personalized plans to help manage work-related stressors, potentially enhancing mental well-being and consequently productivity, when used with empathy and understanding.

Consider Amy, a software engineer caught in the grueling demands of a high-pressure project. The stress began to leak into her digital behavior, altering her typing patterns, mouse movements, and screen time. Her physical health was not spared; noticeable changes in her exercise and sleep patterns were captured through her wearable device. Observing this, **an AI mental health application prompted, "Looks like you are stressed, Amy. Do you want to take a short break? I can also help you with some quick relaxation techniques."** Surprised yet appreciative, Amy accepted the AI's suggestion, took a meditative break, and returned to her tasks feeling recharged and ready to tackle her tasks.

Imagine an AI tool offering similar assistance to a manager struggling with different unexpected team member situations or an employee needing a confidence boost just before a big presentation.

These scenarios remind me of:

Richard Branson's philosophy: **Take care of your employees, and they'll take care of your business.**

Sri Sri Ravi Shankar's quote: **If you can win over your mind, you can win over the whole world.**

Peter Drucker's insight: **The best way to predict the future is to create it.**

Today, technology offers us the power to predict and shape our workplaces, creating an environment that fosters productivity and mentally equips employees to navigate their challenges.

Orchestrating the Corporate Symphony: M&A, Start-Ups, and Workplace Ecosystems

In the words of **Robin Sharma, "Change is hardest at the beginning, messiest in the middle, and best at the end."** This sentiment mirrors the transformation we've witnessed in the global technology landscape over the last few decades. The vibrant mosaic of this landscape consists of bustling tech hubs from Silicon Valley and Bengaluru to emerging hotspots in Africa and Latin America. This picture is continuously evolving, not just in appearance but at its very core. Economic challenges cause some elements to fade while others, bolder and more innovative, fill the gaps.

In this rapid evolution, the digital age has transformed the tools and mediums we use in our work, obliterating the boundary between traditional craftsmanship and modern technology. In this increasingly interconnected world, we are exposed to an array of unprecedented possibilities and unique challenges.

Our role in this revolution is not merely that of bystanders. We are active contributors, helping to shape and modify this fascinating, ever-evolving tableau. As we delve into the intricate patterns of the global work landscape, we find ourselves amidst a captivating dance of change.

One of the most intriguing aspects of this evolution is its distinct manifestations across the globe. To illustrate, as per ***Refinitiv*****, the value of global mergers and acquisitions soared to an astonishing $5.04 trillion in 2021, the highest since 1980**. This constant reshaping of the corporate world, with firms merging and evolving into new entities, consistently alters the very fabric of the business realm.

Consider the blockbuster acquisition of MGM Studios by Amazon in 2021, a deal worth an astounding $8.45 billion.

This bold move displayed Amazon's unwavering ambition to penetrate deeper into the entertainment industry. With MGM's rich legacy of over 4,000 films and 17,000 TV shows, Amazon Prime Video gained an immense treasure trove of content. This was a significant leap for Amazon into the realm of streaming and content creation.

However, such an acquisition had profound implications for the workplaces of both Amazon and MGM. Employees found themselves having to adapt to a new organizational culture, integrate their operations, and align with Amazon's broader ambitions in the entertainment industry.

These large-scale mergers and acquisitions are not just about the confluence of two organizations; they represent a convergence of technology and creativity, a signal of how industries can evolve and adapt in the swiftly changing corporate landscape.

Moreover, they serve as powerful evidence of workforce resilience during the often lengthy and complex mergers and acquisitions (M&A) journey, right up to the deal's consummation. Simultaneously, they highlight the agility and adaptability of employees, who adeptly navigate the significant transitions towards a unified organization.

The cultural incompatibilities add an extra layer of stress on the employees from both sides. The case of Daimler-Benz's merger with Chrysler Corporation serves as a poignant example of an M&A failure due to cultural incompatibility. This merger, which aimed to bring together German engineering precision with American automotive innovation, ultimately faced insurmountable challenges arising from stark cultural differences. The German company valued methodical decision-making and a hierarchical structure while the American company emphasized agility, creativity, and a more decentralized approach.

The result was a clash of cultures, marked by communication breakdowns, resistance to change, and power struggles. Employees on both sides experienced increased stress as they tried to navigate a rapidly evolving corporate landscape with conflicting norms and practices. This cultural disharmony led to operational inefficiencies, failed synergies, and ultimately, financial losses. The merger, once seen as a strategic move to create a global powerhouse, ended up as a cautionary tale about the critical role of cultural compatibility in M&A success.

The T-Mobile-Sprint merger is another example of how, even within the same industry, cultural differences can impact the success of an M&A deal. These examples underscore the importance of recognizing and addressing cultural differences during the M&A process as they can significantly impact the well-being of employees and the overall success of the merger.

Another fascinating chapter in this exhilarating saga is the birth and meteoric rise of start-ups. Like resilient sprouts breaking through the corporate concrete, start-ups bring an influx of vitality and innovation. **Over 4.4 million new businesses were launched in 2020 in the US, according to the US Census Bureau**. This wave of start-ups is not confined to the US; it resonates on a global scale.

Start-ups are infusing the global economy with fresh vitality. They come with bold visions and audacious risk-taking. However, they also introduce a unique brand of intensity. The atmospheres in these nurseries of innovation are electrified by high stakes and long hours. They become crucibles of fierce competition, where youthful exuberance burns intensely. It's within these spaces that personal well-being can, at times, be pushed to the periphery.

Imagine the corporate world as a grand symphony. The fast-growing, innovative companies, buoyed by mergers and acquisitions, are the deep, resonating notes of the cellos and basses – robust, compelling, altering the atmosphere as they reverberate. Start-ups represent the vivacious trills of violins and the lively chirps of flutes, quick, spirited, and dazzling. Together, they compose the contemporary corporate symphony.

Harmonizing the Digital Symphony: Emerging Technologies and Work-Life Balance

What this symphony begets is an emerging world where the boundaries between countries, corporations, and even individuals are growing ever fainter. In this reshaped landscape, innovation has become the currency and agility the lifeblood.

In this symphonic illustration of the modern corporate world, the role of the virtuosic musicians— our employees—has undergone a transformation as they've adapted their rhythms to the beat of "digital transformation." Once primarily the preserve of freelancers, remote work is now the anthem sung by the contemporary workforce. As technology took center stage, it wooed both employees and employers. The former savored newfound flexibility while the latter were able to tap into a global pool of talent. However, when the pandemic struck, the tempo had to be drastically increased, and the world raced to adapt. Living rooms turned into conference rooms, and kitchen tables transformed into office desks. Platforms such as Slack and Zoom became bustling digital workspaces, although devoid of the traditional watercooler chatter.

The transformation wasn't limited to the internal dynamics of corporations; it extended to consumer behavior and expectations as well. Today's consumers demand the entire orchestra to be agile, expecting it to produce more innovative, creative, and personalized melodies. To cater to these dynamically changing demands, numerous organizations have transformed their business models at an unprecedented pace. For example, Starbucks. The pandemic compelled them to limit in-store experiences, leading them to expedite the deployment of mobile ordering, curbside pickup, and contactless payments. Their narrative underscores the significance of embracing change and capitalizing on the digital wave.

The crowning piece in this intricate orchestra is **connectivity**. We inhabit not just a connected world but one that thrives in hyper-connectivity. Our colleagues might be thousands of miles away, but they're just a Zoom call away. This global landscape has business operating at warp speed, compressing our vast planet into what feels more like a close-knit community. Yet, with this deep-seated connectivity comes a formidable responsibility — the relentless pressure to always be "on."

As we traverse the transformative labyrinths and the ensuing **always-on** pressure of the digital era, something even more intriguing looms on the horizon. Picture a robot performing your job or a machine learning model mimicking your boss's decision-making. This isn't a plot from a science fiction novel but a reality in the era of artificial intelligence (AI) and automation.

Let's delve into how these technological marvels are shaping the global work landscape.

Firstly, let's acquaint ourselves with our new coworkers—the robots. Their realm isn't confined to car assembly lines anymore; they're integrated into our offices, hospitals, and even homes. For instance, AI chatbots of Salesforce and Zoho have revolutionized customer service and support and are currently being further evolved with GenAI use cases. Yet, every innovative leap brings about significant disruption. AI's efficiency makes it a boon for businesses, but it raises a pressing question: What becomes of the human workforce in this new landscape? The case of bank tellers, once a staple in every bank branch and a role my mother played for many years, now obsolete with the advent of digital ledgers and automated cash counters, is a stark reminder of this shift.

Next, we shift our focus to **data**. Amid the vast ocean of the digital age, data is the most coveted treasure. Astute businesses don't merely accumulate data, they engage with it. They leverage data to make decisions that are precise, informed, and almost prophetic. Netflix, for example, scrutinizes viewing patterns, ratings, and searches to not just recommend shows but to also decide what shows to produce.

The advent of **5G** takes center stage here. If data is the treasure, then 5G is the high-speed ship that whisks you to it in record time. Tasks that once took hours to analyze can now be executed almost instantaneously. This breakthrough doesn't just speed up operations, it revolutionizes how businesses respond to trends, challenges, and opportunities. Take the case of autonomous vehicles that rely on data and 5G to make real-time decisions, potentially lifesaving ones.

However, every coin has two sides. As this digital ecosystem densifies, it provides hackers with new crevices to exploit and launch increasingly sophisticated attacks. Imagine the stress on an IT manager, whose treasure trove comprises invaluable data. A single breach can sink the ship, leaving employees, especially those at the helm, under immense pressure to navigate these treacherous waters safely. My memory harks back to Christmas week of 2021 when our IT team put in heroic efforts to remediate Log4J issues. **Cybersecurity** has become one of the top priorities of most organizations.

As we move through the trajectories of AI, automation, data, 5G, and cybersecurity, we encounter a landscape that is exhilarating yet often unsettling. This transition, while enhancing efficiency and accuracy, has also introduced its own set of anxieties. The digital revolution has reshaped our roles, necessitating us to reskill and adapt to new technologies, reflecting the global trend. The parts we play in this new world aren't merely defined by our job titles but by our capacity to adapt, learn, and evolve. Amidst these changes, the concept of work-life balance has undergone a radical transformation, akin to overhauling a garden. Today's professionals aren't merely nurturing a single tree; they're tending to a diverse ecosystem and cultivating various flora to cater to different needs.

Resonating Repercussions: Pulse of Productivity

A pivotal catalyst in this shift is the changing perception of time, exemplified by **Tim Ferriss's *The 4-Hour Workweek*.** The traditional 9 to 5, five-day week structure suddenly seemed like a relic of the past. The question became: How can I work smarter, not harder?

Take the example of Amazon. A titan now, but back in its early days, Jeff Bezos prioritized finding a balance that accommodated relentless innovation and personal well-being. His advocacy for eight hours of sleep went against the popular narrative of burning the midnight oil. Bezos realized that a balanced lifestyle was key to making game-changing decisions. Contrastingly, we have Elon Musk, whose ambitious endeavors with SpaceX and Tesla border on science fiction. Musk's Herculean work ethic practices are well-known.

The performers in our grand corporate orchestra, with their extraordinary talent and skills, require care for their mental and emotional well-being.

These aspects form the subtle nuances and pitches, enriching the symphony of their work, deserving attention and nurturing. As the symphony's intensity and tempo surge, it falls upon the maestros—the leaders and organizations—to ensure harmony prevails. It's their mandate as well as a huge challenge to keep the symphony from devolving into a cacophony, where dissonant notes of burnout and stress outplay the harmonious melodies of innovation and progress.

According to the **World Health Organization (WHO):**

- **15% of adults of working age suffer from a mental disorder.**
- **Employees with unresolved mental health issues suffer a 35% reduction in productivity.**
- **83% of US workers suffer from work-related stress, with 25% saying their job is the number one stressor in their lives.**
- **30%+ of people don't even know where to go for help.**

Picture an employee burdened by unaddressed mental health issues experiencing a 35% drop in their productivity. This downward spiral does not stop at an individual level; it permeates the office, straining bonds and relationships among colleagues. The cogs in the machine begin to grind against each other. The assembly line isn't merely jamming; it's teetering on the brink of collapse.

Now, envision an anxious worker faced with an overwhelming sea of choices yet lost in the storm. A startling 30% of these individuals are directionless; they don't know where to turn for help or solace. The guiding beacon they desperately need remains obscured by fog.

Looking at the American work landscape, the situation is even more turbulent. The relentless assault of work-related stress engulfs 83% of the workforce. For a quarter of these individuals, their job isn't just a demanding task but a relentless adversary that keeps them perpetually on edge.

Moreover, the burgeoning gig economy has introduced a new set of challenges. A wave of independent contractors, freelancers, and project-based workers are contributing to an increasingly fluid, flexible, and yet volatile labor market. Gig workers often grapple with uncertain incomes, a lack of traditional employment benefits, and the isolation that comes from working outside a conventional team environment. This precariousness can exacerbate feelings of anxiety and instability, further intensifying the mental health pressures faced by today's workforce.

Let this sink in. As per the WHO, globally, an astonishing **12 billion working days are lost each year due to depression and anxiety.** Quantifying this loss, we're looking at **$1 trillion in lost productivity annually.** This isn't a mere chink in the armor; it's a gaping chasm.

Now, it's time for a wake-up call. Mental health isn't just a personal matter; it's the foundation of productivity. You wouldn't put a Formula 1 car on the track without a tune-up, would you? The human brain requires similar maintenance and pit stops.

> A technology leader whom I deeply admire once confessed his struggle with mental health issues. His decision to take a three-month sabbatical left me stunned. He revealed this over dinner, explaining his need to prioritize mental well-being.
>
> My initial reaction was far from commendable. I failed to grasp the severity of his mental health challenges, largely because he always seemed so vibrant and cheerful. I confess, I questioned the legitimacy of his admission, a response I now deeply regret, perhaps forever.

Had his ailment been physical, my empathy would have been natural and immediate. However, because his struggles were mental and not seen visibly, I failed to be empathetic of the situation. This was a profound wake-up call about the often invisible severity of mental health issues, even among successful leaders.

This experience radically altered my approach towards my team. Mental well-being now takes precedence in my leadership style. When this leader returned from his sabbatical, I noticed a remarkable enhancement in his focus and effortlessness, further solidifying my newfound understanding of mental health's influence on performance.

Let's broaden the lens now. Imagine the cascading effect of such mental health revelations on an organization's landscape. It's not just about efficiency or growth; it's also about that invaluable bond with customers. A nurtured mind is a wellspring of creativity and empathy, and it's through these attributes that brands forge lasting connections with their customers. After all, employee experience impacts customer experience!

Indeed, many employers are reaching out with supportive measures, such as providing coverage for psychological consultations and supporting many employee assistance programs (EAP). However, isn't this akin to applying a bandage after a wound has become septic? The dawn of a new approach needs to break, one that's more preemptive.

Crescendo of Care: Towards Predictive and Precisive Well-Being

Imagine a workspace where mental well-being isn't an afterthought but forms the bedrock of every policy. Imagine a world where technology plays a supportive role in customizing and personalizing mental fitness plans for each individual. Envision a reality where human resources (HR) isn't just a department but an ethos permeating every hallway, workstation, and coffee break.

The future workforce is stepping up its demands. They aren't making requests but assertions.

As per the American Psychological Association (APA's) Work and Well-being Survey, a majority (81%) of survey respondents said that employers' support for mental health will be an important consideration when they look for work in the future.

This isn't just about today's skirmishes; it's about fortifying the strongholds for future battles.

So, what's at stake? It's the very foundation upon which our industries are built. The call to action is clear—organizations that sow seeds of empathy and mindfulness within their core structure not only nurture happier employees but also cultivate lasting legacies.

In an age of incessant notifications, emails, and pings, mental health is both the shield and the sword, determining whether one emerges victorious or vanquished on the corporate battlefield.

The time has come for both companies and individuals to gear up for battle. Equip your teams—not just with technology but also with a sound mind. Mental health programs, counseling, mindfulness training—these are not indulgences; they are necessary resources.

Technology, a powerful force that can either enable or subjugate, brings a flood of complications, from the struggle to stay relevant to the fading lines between the digital and the physical realms. As such, our mental strength becomes the compass guiding us through these tumultuous waters. It's not just about leveraging the power of technology but also about protecting the essence of our humanity. To prosper in this exciting era, let's arm ourselves with knowledge and resilience. With mental well-being as our anchor and innovation as our sail, we can navigate both storms and calm waters in pursuit of unseen horizons.

What if we could predict the storm and reinforce our defenses in advance?

Imagine an organization that doesn't wait for the armor to break but regularly maintains and strengthens it, thereby preventing the crack in the first place and creating an impregnable shield. Imagine a world where even the subtle signs of a chink in one's armor are not just detected but met with empathy and care. This alliance between technology and humanity could signify the beginning of workspaces that are not just productivity hubs but sanctuaries of holistic well-being.

This is where the concept of **predictive well-being** comes in, a period where employers and employees collaborate to establish a workspace that constantly monitors, nurtures, and bolsters mental health. In this reality, we could harness technology, particularly AI, to devise personalized mental health management plans based on real-time data and individual insights. Picture an intuitive assistant, an AI-powered companion, which enables individuals to manage their mental health and grow stronger each day.

The ocean ahead is vast and uncharted, with waves that challenge us and invite us forward. As we embark on this journey, let's be more than explorers and navigators. Let's harness technology as a tool to preserve the essence of our humanity—our minds and spirits. With our mental well-being secured and our minds alert, we can harness the winds of change and innovation, discovering not only new territories but also our own boundless potential.

Chapter Summary

- The rapid advancement of connectivity, automation, AI, data, and 5G technology is transforming the global work landscape, requiring the workforce to adapt and evolve continuously.
- This digital revolution is leading to unintended job-related stress and mental health issues, creating a hidden crisis within the workforce.
- As we sail through the digital era, it's critical to maintain a balance between technological innovation and mental well-being, ensuring we not only survive but thrive in this new landscape.
- Mental health significantly affects productivity, with serious implications for individuals, businesses, and customers. It's no longer just a personal matter.
- Traditional measures to address mental health in the workplace, such as covering for psychological consultations, are reactive and inadequate.
- There is increasing expectation from employees for their employers to provide robust mental health support as a standard part of their work package.
- The future workplace needs to be a sanctuary of holistic well-being, where mental health is prioritized and nurtured proactively.
- Leveraging technology and AI, we have the opportunity to make workplaces move towards a proactive approach and predictive mental well-being of their employees.

Chapter 2

Burning Bright, Not Out: Overcoming Burnout in a Competitive World

The contemporary global workspace, sprawling and vibrant, is not a realm for the complacent. Merely surviving is not sufficient; it requires excellence. The very factors that stimulate significant expansion and success are the same that introduce unparalleled trials. **The opportunities are immense, but they bring with them their own unique set of hurdles.**

In this competitive environment, professionals are influenced and shaped by their adversities, much like a piece of iron in a blacksmith's hands. The pressures they confront play a key role in sculpting them, similar to the way a smith molds a sword in his forge.

Consider a novice stepping into the world of finance on Wall Street. It's a place pulsing with ambition, where every stock market tick could spell fortune or failure. As a newcomer to the industry, his experience is limited, but Wall Street serves as a crucible, shaping and refining him. The intensity of this environment hones his skills. He learns to maneuver with the changing numbers and fluidity of the markets and ultimately metamorphoses into a complex human algorithm adept at assessing risks and making forecasts. This isn't merely a physical change; it's a mental and emotional evolution as well, filled with challenges, competition, and a bit of luck.

Picture an aspiring entrepreneur in Nairobi. Here, the hurdles are more palpable—systemic obstacles, resource scarcity, and a race against time. Nonetheless, her entrepreneurial zeal and innovative concepts act as both the heat and the anvil, shaping her into a proficient businesswoman and a catalyst for change.

Think of a consultant moving from servicing one customer to another in a short span of time, thriving to add value to the customer by leveraging his skills and experience of working with multiple customers, handling high levels of stress, traveling to customer locations 50%+ of the time, most of the time Monday through Thursday, eating out, sleeping in new places, and managing the highly demanding customer environment

These professionals face a variety of intricate and diverse challenges. But what they share is resilience, grit, and the willpower to rise above their difficulties and mold themselves into masters in their respective fields.

Inspired by ***Malcolm Gladwell's 10,000-hour rule***, we comprehend that mastery isn't an overnight phenomenon; it's the outcome of consistent, diligent effort over an extended period. The Beatles, for example, didn't achieve stardom overnight; it was the result of their extensive performance period in Hamburg. Similarly, **Bill Gates** didn't conjure Microsoft out of thin air; his early encounters with computers at the Computer Center Corporation laid the groundwork for his journey.

The Unending Marathon of Fierce Competition: Talent, Timing, and Tenacity

Success in the professional world for each individual is a blend of talent, opportunity, and relentless effort. Their knowledge and skills, analogous to weapons in a battle, are honed amidst the blazing trials of their unique challenges. These trials temper them while each misstep and late-night work session molds their trajectory. However, this process isn't devoid of risks. The extreme conditions that shape professionals can also inundate them, posing potential threats to their well-being.

This leads us to the question: **How do these professionals manage to excel without succumbing to the pressure that comes with their development?** As we delve into this, we find ourselves in a scenario reminiscent of an unending marathon, propelled by the swift strides of technological advancements.

In this marathon, technology serves as the pacesetter, accelerating the rhythm of work and life. The era when competition was limited to a neighboring coworker or city is long past; technology has broadened the scope to include the entire planet. A newer but significant player in this marathon is artificial intelligence, an advancement so potent that it almost carries a veil of magic, Capable of performing tasks traditionally requiring human intellect and manual labor while never tiring or needing rest. However, as AI appears to sprint effortlessly, human professionals often find themselves gasping to maintain pace.

This dynamic leads to a situation where tools designed to boost human capabilities can feel like formidable competitors, escalating the pressure to outpace not just human counterparts but advanced algorithms as well. This unrelenting competition can exert substantial pressure on our most crucial resource: the human mind.

The impact on mental health in the global workspace can echo the fatigue experienced by marathon runners. This weariness can cultivate a sense of pressure and mental fog, often escorted by anxiety, a frequent associate of those attempting to keep stride in a perpetually evolving professional landscape. Additionally, the stress of constant connectivity, where work persistently infringes upon personal space through unending notifications, can blur the boundaries between professional and personal life.

Yet, even in the most intense scenarios, the importance of balance cannot be overlooked. The human spirit is robust, but it also necessitates renewal. In the realm of professional life, the most skilled individuals are those who comprehend the significance of pacing themselves. They acknowledge that occasional slowdown can enhance their performance over the long run.

The pressure to perform and evolve professionally is not intrinsically harmful. It could be one of the catalysts for personal as well as professional growth. However, amidst the dynamic progress and competition, we should not lose sight of our fundamental human traits—heart and mind—that no AI can emulate (*at least, not yet!*).

When scrutinizing this high-velocity professional environment, it may occasionally seem as if professionals are tirelessly sprinting, their faces taut with determination, but they appear stationary. It's as if they're on a treadmill beneath a relentless spotlight, perpetually in motion yet rooted in the same place.

When the Sun Doesn't Set: The Always-On Hustle Culture

In the contemporary work environment, the traditional boundaries between day and night, work and leisure, have blurred. The tools of the modern workspace—emails, messages, video calls—operate beyond the constraints of time zones.

Imagine a scenario where you're seated at the dinner table, surrounded by family and enticing food, only to be interrupted by a work notification. A client in a different corner of the globe, where it's now daybreak, needs an immediate update on an infra outage. This intrusion is symptomatic of an ever-present work culture that persistently encroaches upon personal time.

While the capability to be incessantly connected and productive may initially seem empowering, it also carries its downsides. The human mind necessitates intervals of rest to recharge and perform optimally. However, in an ever-present work culture, the mind often functions akin to a machine devoid of an off switch, perpetually engaged, even during the hours meant for rest.

To illustrate, I once managed a scrum team working on a critical SaaS transformation project. More than 60% of the team was recruited in the last two years when remote work had become the norm, allowing us to access talent anywhere in the world. The ten-member scrum team spanned five different time zones, compelling everyone to extend their work hours just to synchronize efficiently. We eventually had to strategize location allocation for the pods to minimize the number of time zones and manage the work-life balance.

This ceaseless pressure to perform in dynamic environments can have serious implications for mental health. Anxiety becomes an uninvited and perpetual companion as individuals grapple to balance immediate duties with looming tasks. The endless onslaught of notifications further fragments concentration, creating an atmosphere of sustained stress.

Without spaces for rest and disconnection, opportunities for moments of joy and introspection become rare, much like stars obscured by the incessant city lights. The repercussions of this relentless work culture frequently manifest as burnout, a state of emotional, physical, and mental exhaustion caused by excessive and prolonged stress. It's essential, therefore, to recognize the signs of burnout and to cultivate strategies for managing and preventing it in the hustle of the ever-present work culture.

Understanding Burnout: Symptoms and Causes

According to ZIPPIA RESEARCH:

- **89% of workers have experienced burnout within the past year.**

21% of workers say their company does not offer any program to help alleviate burnout.

- **The burnout rate is 59% as of 2022, which is up 13.5% from 2021.**

Do you ever feel like a superhero, constantly saving the day without a break? You may not be the only one! If so, you might be headed towards **burnout,** a state of exhaustive physical, emotional, and mental fatigue, usually found in people persistently stressed or overworked. The initial symptoms of burnout might often be subtle, but over time, they become increasingly noticeable. Recognizing these signs and taking proactive steps is crucial in preventing or managing burnout.

Consider the following:

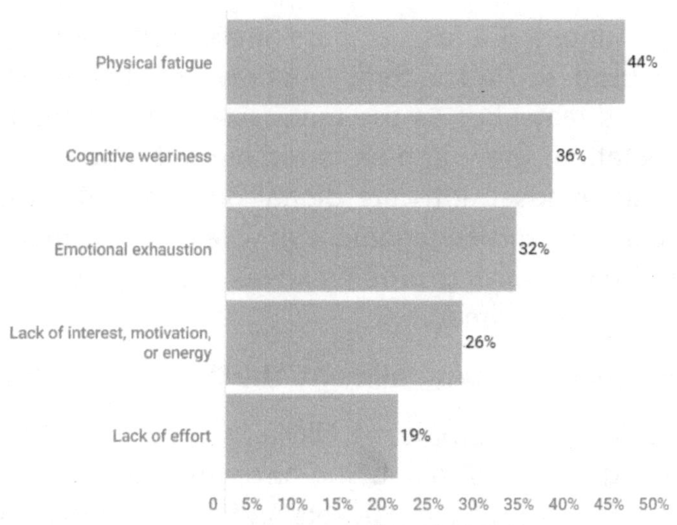

- **Physical Exhaustion: More Than Just Being Tired**

  Let's consider the case of James, a software engineer at a rapidly growing tech start-up. Once known for his endless energy and drive, James started noticing an overwhelming sense of fatigue creeping into his day-to-day life due to the speed-to-market urgency of the platform features he was working on. This wasn't the kind of tiredness a weekend sleep-in could fix; it was as if the exhaustion had seeped into his very core, making even the simplest tasks feel like uphill battles.

- **Insomnia: When Rest Becomes Unreachable**

  Then there's Amelia, a program manager overseeing several digital transformation initiatives. Despite her best efforts to maintain a work-life balance, she found herself lying awake at night, haunted by endless to-do lists, project timelines, and better collaboration tactics amongst the execution teams. Her mind, overloaded and weary, ironically became too restless to switch off, turning her nights into extensions of her workday's degraded productivity, quality, concentration, and problem-solving abilities.

- **Loss of Enthusiasm: The "Why Bother" Syndrome**

  Think about Carlos, a passionate cybersecurity analyst who used to find a thrill in unraveling the most intricate digital threats. But as the team size reduced, workload and expectations grew, and he found himself slipping into a "why bother" mindset. Intricate digital puzzles that once sparked his curiosity and engagement now felt like an unending slog. The thrill of solving problems was replaced with a sense of obligation and dread.

- **Inadequacy and Unfulfillment: The Unconquerable Mountain**

  Consider the example of Olivia, a seasoned data scientist working for a tech giant. She once reveled in the complexity of her job, using vast datasets and newer models to unravel trends and insights. However, as her projects grew more demanding due to changing data sets, and deadlines more stringent, the models she was creating weren't very successful, and she began feeling a persistent sense of ineffectiveness and unfulfillment. Olivia felt like she was perpetually climbing a mountain that only grew steeper with each step, causing her to question her capabilities and worth.

Now, let's delve into the prevalent factors that contribute to employee burnout:

- **Overwhelming Workload: The Endless Juggling Act**

  Picture Alex, a software engineer in a bustling tech firm. As his team rushes to meet the launch deadline of a new app, his to-do list balloons out of proportion. With each passing day, new tasks pile onto old ones, turning his professional life into a ceaseless juggling act. Such an overwhelming workload is a significant trigger for burnout in tech professionals, who often grapple with aggressive timelines and high-stakes projects.

- **Lack of Control: The Passenger's Plight**

  Meet Janet, a product manager who is facing conflicting priorities. She feels she has lost control over her projects, the work pace, and ultimately, her career trajectory. She's akin to a passenger in her own professional life, watching someone else steer the wheel while she's carried along the unknown road. The feeling of having no control frequently intensified in high-speed tech atmospheres, can significantly contribute to burnout.

- **Insufficient Rewards: The Unmet Expectations**

  Take the case of Martin, a cybersecurity expert who's been putting in extra hours to thwart the latest wave of cyberattacks. Despite his efforts, he finds his monetary compensation, recognition, or appreciation lacking. The feeling of not receiving deserved rewards can breed frustration and resentment, pushing tech professionals like Martin towards the precipice of burnout.

- **Lack of Social Support: The Isolation in the Crowd**

  Emma, a remote web developer, yearns for the casual camaraderie and watercooler conversations that once peppered her workday. The shift to remote work has led to isolation, and the absence of these shared moments of relaxation can severely impact morale and motivation, thus leading to burnout. Lack of social support might further lead to prolonged feelings of loneliness, detachment, and reduced motivation, which can certainly exacerbate stress levels and potentially lead to other mental health issues over time.

- **Value Conflict: The Clash of Purpose**

  Lastly, there's Sam, a technologist in a leading AI company. He joined the company to use AI for social good, but the recent shift in the company's focus towards profit over purpose has caused a deep value conflict. The discord between personal beliefs and the tasks or goals pursued at work can drain the sense of fulfillment, pushing professionals like Sam towards burnout.

A Personal Encounter with Burnout: An Eye-Opener

During a pivotal period in my career, I was teetering on the edge of a high-ranking partnership role amidst a whirlwind of daunting tasks. I was spearheading digital transformation initiatives for multiple clients, which demanded innovative strategies, nurturing a blossoming team, and continually striving to deliver unprecedented value. Striving for accelerated growth, I found myself balancing complex, multiple customer deliverables and managing my expanding team while also seeking to add significant value to my portfolio. The relentless pace of work seeped into my life, subtly chipping away at my physical and emotional resilience. Months flew by, blurring into a frenzied pattern of endless work. Sleep had become a luxury that I could barely afford, and regular meals became optional, lost in the ceaseless rhythm of my work life.

It took a harrowing seizure and a subsequent hospital stay to jolt me out of this self-destructive spiral. While deciphering my lifestyle habits for my doctors, seeking to unravel the cause of my condition, I was struck by a sudden realization. For months on end, I had been precariously wading through burnout, oblivious to the toll it was taking on me. This realization was as much a diagnosis as it was a wake-up call.

Looking back, my children confessed that they had been silently observing my deteriorating health. However, their tender age held them back from expressing their worries. It served as a reminder that those close to us often detect the subtle signs of burnout that we tend to overlook.

Regaining my health and equilibrium was not easy; it was punctuated by years of medication. It was a profound lesson in introspection and the importance of harmonious living. Gradually, I learned to balance my professional responsibilities with my personal well-being. I embraced wholesome habits and practiced mindfulness, eventually reaching a point where I could discontinue my medication.

The encounter with burnout was a daunting yet invaluable chapter of my life. It underscored the significance of a well-rounded work-life balance. This hard-learned lesson is now an integral part of my life, a beacon guiding me towards conscious, mindful living and working.

Burnout Beyond Borders: A Global Tech Workforce Strain

Let's consider the widespread nature of burnout, particularly within the global tech workforce.

When examining the landscape of burnout, it isn't just a lone figure we see against the sunset; rather, it's a vast congregation of weary figures spanning the globe. Listening carefully, the chorus of countless exhausted voices resonates, indicating that burnout is a growing global phenomenon.

- According to a 2018 Gallup study, **23% of employees reported feeling burned out at work very often or always,** while **an additional 44% reported feeling burned out sometimes.** That's about two-thirds of the workforce! It's akin to seeing two out of three ships embarking on a voyage but taking on water.

  Fast forward to 2020, when the world was gripped by the COVID-19 pandemic. A monster wave rocked our ships. Remote work, once a novelty, became the norm. While the boundaries between work and home blurred, the workday stretched.

  - According to the **National Bureau of Economic Research, the average workday lengthened by 48.5 minutes** during the early weeks of the pandemic. The canvas of global work culture was furiously repainted.
  - The **World Health Organization,** recognizing the gravity of the issue, included burnout in its 11th Revision of the International Classification of Diseases (ICD-11) as an occupational phenomenon. In essence, the WHO illuminated this pervasive issue, officially acknowledging its prevalence and impact.

It's crucial to note that this is not just a Western issue. It's a global concern. For instance, in Japan, they have the term ***karoshi,*** meaning death due to overwork. This isn't a metaphor; it's a tragically literal occurrence. Meanwhile, in South Korea, the government had to intervene to limit the maximum work hours per week from 68 to 52 due to excessively long working hours.

Furthermore, this issue does not discriminate by age. Millennials, often tagged as the "burnout generation," are profoundly impacted. A 2018 Deloitte study reported that **84% of millennials experienced some degree of burnout at their current job.**

The realm of burnout is like a hall of mirrors, reflecting the exhaustion of tech professionals from all corners of the globe. It's not an individual issue; it's a collective one. It echoes in the restless typing of engineers, the hushed frustrations of data analysts, the long virtual meetings of program managers, and the sleepless nights of tech support teams.

The Quest for Balance: Conquering Endless Hours in a Competitive Realm

As we journey through the tangled web of prolonged hours and unrelenting competition, it's vividly apparent that we're in dire need of sustainable strategies. Our mental health is hanging in the balance, and akin to voyagers heading into uncharted territory, we must be well-equipped. Let's delve into some actionable measures, akin to a survival kit, to navigate this 21st-century maze of workplace competition.

- **Conquer the Sands of Time**

  The first step to balance is gaining control of your time. The modern workplace can feel like quicksand—the more you struggle, the deeper you sink. Establish firm boundaries. When the workday ends, let it truly end. Prevent work commitments from invading your personal time. This is the lifeline that pulls you from the engulfing sands of constant work. Strive for the balance between strict task lists and spontaneous creativity, between control and freedom. Harnessing the sands of time is about balance, not a constant struggle against the current.

- **Believe in Balance**

  Embrace the belief that success, work, and personal well-being can harmoniously coexist. It's a common misconception that success requires extreme hard work at the expense of personal well-being. The reality is that everyone has a unique equilibrium between these aspects of life. By discovering our individual balance and establishing sustainable habits and rhythms, we can achieve a holistic, fulfilling life. Remember, a happy life is a successful one.

- **Strength in Numbers**

  Here's a comforting truth—you're not traversing this wilderness solo. Your colleagues, friends, and family members are journeying alongside you. When was the last time you had a long and casual conversation with your colleague outside of work topics? These bonds form the social adhesive that uplifts morale. Consider it as establishing a communal campfire—the light, warmth, and security are amplified in a group.

- **Activate Zen Mode**

  Visualize a serene pond nestled in the heart of a bustling forest—this image of tranquility embodies the essence of mindfulness and meditation. Just a few moments of quiet introspection can extinguish the wildfires of stress. And the beauty of it? You have an array of digital tools to guide you on this journey. Emphasize the fact that the world does not revolve around us. We are only a minuscule particle in this world. Cultivate some level of spirituality. It's okay to take time off, to truly enjoy life. Most importantly, let go of guilt when you do. Embrace the calm of the Zen mode, and it can transform your life.

- **Unleash Your Creative Spirit**

  Remember the adage, "All work and no play make Jack a dull boy." The contemporary workspace thrives on the lifeblood of creativity. Indulge in art, dance, writing, or engage in any activity that ignites your spirit. That's your dose of vitamin "C"—creativity. Consider it your protective shield against burnout.

- **Embrace Guidance**

  The professional labyrinth is vast and complex. Occasionally, you'll need a seasoned guide. Don't hesitate to reach out to mental health professionals. They are the experienced pathfinders who can help you steer through the most intricate terrain.

- **Nurture the Physical Self**

  Lastly, remember your body is the steadfast vehicle maneuvering through this wilderness. It necessitates care and maintenance. Regular sleep, exercise, and balanced meals are the necessary pit stops it requires.

This modern-day jungle of workplace competition is not only about survival but also about triumph. It's about turning the heat into mettle, transforming pressure into performance. It's about striking the right balance between resilience and rest, ambition and introspection. It's about choosing wisely, choosing health.

Consider this saying by Sri Sri Ravi Shankar: **"The Mind has two abilities, one is to focus, the other is to expand and relax."**

The idea is not just to make it through but to emerge stronger, more balanced, and more fulfilled. It's not just about the battle but the spoils of war—the gratification, the growth, the glory.

In this evolving scenario, our decisions serve as the craft tools shaping our professional journey. The harmony we strike between our aspirations and values carves the quality of our professional existence. Every decision, every adjustment, and every victory in boundary-setting or deriving satisfaction from our work shapes our overall professional persona. The objective is not just to survive amidst challenges but to know when to retreat and recuperate.

> **If you feel "burnout" setting in, if you feel demoralized and exhausted, it is best, for the sake of everyone, to withdraw and restore yourself.**
>
> **—Dalai Lama**

Burnout isn't the sole tempest looming large; the specter of job insecurity darkens the horizon. But what if this storm, too, could be transformed into a navigable challenge rather than an overwhelming force? Dive into Chapter 3 as we tackle the VUCA-fueled reality head-on, armed with **adaptability, continuous learning, networking, emotional intelligence, innovation, personal brand, and self-belief**.

Chapter Summary

- The traditional boundaries between work and leisure have blurred due to the rise of global connectivity and an always-on work culture.
- The constant pressure to perform and lack of rest in today's work environment can lead to burnout—a state of exhaustive physical, emotional, and mental fatigue.
- Symptoms of burnout include profound physical exhaustion, insomnia, a loss of enthusiasm, and feelings of inadequacy and unfulfillment.
- Causes of burnout can include an overwhelming workload, a lack of control, insufficient rewards, a lack of social support, and value conflict.
- Burnout is a prevalent and growing issue worldwide. About two-thirds of the workforce experiences burnout to some degree
- It's essential to take proactive steps to prevent or manage burnout. This includes setting boundaries, fostering social connections, practicing mindfulness, nurturing creativity, seeking professional help when needed, and taking care of one's physical health.
- The goal in the modern workplace should be not only to thrive amidst challenges but also to know when to step back and recover.
- Mental and physical well-being should be prioritized as much as achievements.

Chapter 3

Sailing Through Rough Seas: Taming the Waves of Job Insecurity

Navigating the path of uncharted technological progress is like steering a ship through a wild sea of ceaseless innovation. In many ways, it mirrors the epoch of the 1800s, where the introduction of steam power heralded the dawn of the Industrial Revolution. Both eras are laced with **challenges**, **change**, and the enduring need for **adaptability**.

In this tech arena, job insecurity isn't just a buzzword—it's a VUCA-fueled reality (volatility, uncertainty, complexity, and ambiguity). The pace of change in this digital age isn't a gentle breeze but a turbulent tornado, reshaping landscapes overnight. Job roles that once stood firm are now ephemeral, and career trajectories resemble dynamic mazes. Yet, within this chaos, lies a thrilling paradox: Volatility creates not just challenges, but opportunities, too. The heartbeat of the tech insecurity isn't just change, it's the rhythm of evolution itself. Embrace this uncertainty, for every twist holds the seed of opportunity, waiting to be harnessed by the brave and the agile.

Take my journey as a software developer, for instance. The evolution of my career path is a clear reflection of these transformational tides. As a C++ developer in my early days, I found my world upended when Java, like a dazzling meteor, entered the programming universe with huge marketing hype. While switching from C++ to Java was really easy for me, C programmer peers struggled with an ominous sense of obsolescence, trying to understand the object-oriented concept and newer ways of programming—a feeling synonymous with job insecurity.

Just when we began to regain our footing, another wave hit us. The outsourcing trend was gathering momentum. As a technology consultant in the US, this stirred my fears of job insecurity. We had to navigate not only the potential offshore shift of our roles but also grapple with the reality of transferring our hard-earned knowledge to our counterparts from drastically different cultural backgrounds. My senior leaders were worried that their revenues would go down with the increase in offshoring. These concerns were later proven unwarranted!

Of course, the technology tides are not the only ones causing job insecurity. Many other factors contribute to the storm, including M&As, globalization, and the constant battle between high-cost and best-cost locations. The recent wave of layoffs and haphazard resource planning further agitate the turbulent waters of our career seas, causing job insecurity to swell.

Yet, if we stop and think for a moment—had every forecast of job insecurity come true, wouldn't over half the workforce be jobless today? That's clearly not the reality.

Many of us have ridden the wave of technology, acclimatized to the shifting work paradigms, and successfully navigated choppy waters to promising careers. **So, while the storm seems bigger, it's crucial to see job insecurity as a transitory storm that can be weathered, not an immovable monolith. Also, acceptance of the trend, as opposed to resistance, opens up solutions!**

As technology gallops on, roles morph, and work practices evolve, it's our mental agility, strategic planning, and proactive action that become our life raft, navigating us towards a secure and successful career. However, it's crucial to acknowledge that the repercussions of job insecurity extend beyond economic concerns—they touch the realm of mental well-being, impacting individuals and their families.

The University of Manchester cites ***job insecurity as a significant factor in heightened anxiety, depression, and overall well-being decline***.

Take for instance, Steve, who started his career as a C developer, embraced Java when it emerged, explored powerful features of PHP during its early days, switched to Python as the language rose in prominence, and is now a sought-after AI/ML developer. Despite experiencing two major layoffs due to organizational restructuring and an M&A, he remained resilient, quite active on LinkedIn, and has lately become instrumental in the growth of a couple of start-ups. Steve's journey exemplifies the adaptability, resilience, and foresight necessary in today's fluid workplace. He is like a chameleon, skillfully blending into his changing environment, always relevant, successful, and in demand.

What's his secret? How did Steve stay ahead, navigate the stormy seas of job insecurity, and remain not just afloat but at the helm? The answers lie in seven different aspects:

Adaptability, continuous learning, networking, emotional intelligence, innovation, and personal brand, with all of these underpinned by one MAGIC ingredient—self-belief.

So, buckle up as we embark on a voyage to unravel these key elements and learn how to tame the waves of job insecurity.

1. The Art of Adaptability: Phoenix Rising

The first stride in Steve's journey wasn't about mastering a new set of skills; it was about adopting a resilient mindset and the ability to change the setbacks into stepping stones toward success—**a phoenix mindset**.

This mentality embodies a spirit of resilience, embracing change with a readiness to rise from any challenges encountered along the way. It fosters an unyielding curiosity and a constant willingness to adapt and reinvent oneself, fully acknowledging the ever-evolving landscape of the professional world. Just as Steve recognized, in the dynamic realm of the modern workplace, staying stagnant is not an option. Instead, the phoenix mindset encourages continuous growth and transformation, enabling individuals to soar to new heights despite the winds of change.

Cultural Adaptation: Thriving in the Global Landscapes

Amidst interconnected professional landscapes, cultural agility stands paramount. It involves navigating diverse cultural norms within multicultural teams or foreign environments. This adaptability not only fuels better communication, innovation, and problem-solving but also serves as a buffer against job insecurity. It fosters mutual knowledge exchange, enriching workplaces and broadening global market insights. Embracing change as an avenue for growth, much like Steve's approach, transforms cultural adaptation into an exciting expedition.

2. Mastering the Art of Continuous Learning: Enhancing the Value

Much like a resplendent phoenix rising from its ashes in a blaze of transformation, the spectrum of knowledge holds boundless possibilities. Steve, with a phoenix-like spirit, embraced continuous learning as a powerful catalyst for personal and professional growth. Immersing himself fearlessly in the pursuit of new languages and cutting-edge skills, he soared to new heights by attending webinars, devouring extensive readings, and enrolling in courses on emerging trends. I wouldn't be surprised if Steve is already experimenting with generative AI use cases and preparing himself for the next seismic shift in technology, considering his track record of evolving with the newer technologies as and when they arrived.

The art of continuous learning, akin to the phoenix's transformative rebirth, continuously enhances one's value, in the ever-changing terrain of today's job market.

Unleashing Potential

Consider continuous learning as your passport to perpetual growth. It empowers transformation by ensuring that your knowledge stays relevant in tandem with the latest industry trends. It propels you beyond limits, equipping you with a dynamic skill set to navigate an ever-shifting landscape. Just as technology evolves, so should your expertise. Embrace this journey not as a burden but as a pathway to unlocking your full potential.

Embrace the Student Within

To master continuous learning, foster an unceasing hunger for knowledge. Develop a student mindset that seeks insights from every encounter and experience. Embrace curiosity and relish the act of exploring new realms. Harness digital platforms, courses, and mentorships to expand your horizons. These resources are your treasure trove, offering tailored learning experiences that sharpen your skill set.

Elevating Your Journey

In essence, mastering the art of continuous learning elevates your professional journey to new heights. It's a commitment to perpetual advancement, not merely in technical skills but in adaptability, creativity, and problem-solving. Embrace this journey, for it's a transformative force that unlocks doors to innovation and enduring success.

3. Building a Robust Support System: Leveraging Connections

A solid network of connections, both personal and professional, can act as a safety net during periods of job insecurity. Such a robust support system extends beyond providing emotional and moral support—it can also open up new career opportunities.

Fostering Crucial Networks

In the throes of job insecurity, professional networks emerge as lifelines. They unveil potential job openings, dispense pragmatic career insights, and hold potential as impactful references. Attend networking events, engage with industry groups, and sustain bonds with former colleagues to nurture these connections.

Harness online platforms like LinkedIn, specialized forums, and social media for expansive networking. They connect you globally, bestow insights from others' journeys, and keep you abreast of global industry currents.

Recall the adage: "**To go fast, go alone; to go far, go together**." Forge your network and witness your growth. In times of uncertainty, networks are your anchor to success.

Cultivating Personal Bonds

Personal relationships lay the foundation of your support network. Family and friends offer invaluable emotional sustenance, guiding you through the tempest of stress and ambiguity. Dedicate time and energy to acquainting yourself with colleagues, grasping their backgrounds, and fostering these bonds. Express gratitude by reciprocating the support they extend.

Visualize this backing as the wind beneath your wings. It's not merely about having a circle; it's about possessing a tribe genuinely vested in your triumph. These are colleagues who celebrate your wins, however modest, and friends who lend an ear when the path gets rugged. This unified reservoir of goodwill doesn't merely cushion falls; it propels you towards soaring heights.

Guidance from Mentors

In times of uncertainty, mentors offer guidance, wisdom, and motivation. They share experiences, illuminate pathways, and provide unbiased advice. If a mentor isn't already part of your journey, seek one within your industry or field.

Think of mentorship as a vital lighthouse in stormy waters. Mentors have journeyed these routes before, armed with a treasury of experiences. Their insights can be the line between stumbling and navigating skillfully. Seek mentors aligned with your values and vision. Growth isn't just about climbing; it's about personal evolution.

Remember, mentorship isn't a one-way street. Guiding others also enriches mentors' learning journeys. As they impart knowledge, their perspectives evolve and their leadership skills deepen. The mentor-mentee bond nurtures a reciprocal exchange, fueling continuous learning and growth for both parties. So, as your career advances, embrace mentorship as a chance to give back and uplift others.

4. Cultivating EQ: Unlock Personal and Professional Excellence

Emotional intelligence, often referred to as EQ, is a cornerstone of personal and professional success. It's the ability to understand and manage your emotions while also empathizing with and influencing the emotions of others. In many situations, a simple lapse in EQ leads to huge, negative impacts on relationships as well as on outcomes.

To cultivate emotional intelligence, begin by developing self-awareness. Take time to reflect on your emotions, their triggers, and the impact they have on your decisions and interactions. This self-awareness forms the foundation for understanding how your emotions influence your behavior.

Managing Emotions

Another incredibly important aspect is mastering the skill of self-regulation. This means effectively handling your emotions, particularly in situations where tension is high or stress is present.

It's about steering clear of impulsive reactions and instead nurturing well-considered responses. **Keep in mind this golden rule: DO NOT REACT instinctively. Strive to RESPOND with a composed demeanor in any given circumstance.** Achieving this involves techniques like taking deep breaths, practicing mindfulness, and taking a step back to thoughtfully assess things before taking action.

Empathy is equally vital. It involves genuinely trying to comprehend the emotions and viewpoints of others. To do this, actively listen to what others are saying, imagine yourself in their situation, and showcase your empathy through your actions. These steps can greatly enrich your relationships. Just remember, in order to truly practice empathy, it's important not to let your immediate reactions guide your interactions in the first place.

Social Aptitude

Furthermore, honing social skills is vital. Effective communication, conflict resolution, and teamwork all stem from strong social aptitude. Practicing these skills in different contexts can lead to more harmonious interactions. Also recognize and manage emotional triggers, such as stress or frustration, to maintain your emotional equilibrium. Developing emotional intelligence is a journey of self-discovery, self-regulation, and forging connections built on empathy and effective communication. It's an investment that reaps rewards in both personal and professional realms.

5. Branding YOU: Rise Above the Noise

In today's competitive landscape, personal branding has become more than just a buzzword—it's a strategic imperative. Your personal brand is a reflection of your values, expertise, and unique attributes that set you apart in your field. It's how you're perceived by others, and it plays a significant role in shaping your professional identity. A strong personal brand not only boosts your visibility but also establishes trust, credibility, and influence among peers, potential employers, and clients.

Shaping Your Professional Identity

Building and enhancing your personal brand requires a deliberate and thoughtful approach. Start by defining your unique value proposition—what makes you stand out in your industry? Craft a clear and concise personal mission statement that encapsulates your goals and aspirations. Next, leverage various online platforms to showcase your expertise. Develop a professional and consistent presence on platforms like LinkedIn, where you can share industry insights, engage in meaningful discussions, and demonstrate your thought leadership. **Remember, you ARE unique and so are your experiences and the value you bring to the table.**

Consistency is key—ensure that your personal brand is coherent across all touchpoints, from your online profiles to your offline interactions. Curate your content to align with your brand message and values, positioning yourself as an expert in your field. Engage in networking events, both in person and virtually, to expand your reach and connect with like-minded professionals. Seek opportunities to speak at conferences, write articles, or contribute to discussions related to your expertise. These efforts collectively contribute to bolstering your personal brand and establishing you as a credible authority in your domain.

Remember, personal branding is an ongoing process. Regularly assess and refine your brand, adapting it to your evolving skills and goals. **Authenticity is paramount**—your personal brand should authentically represent who you are and what you bring to the table. By investing in your personal brand, you're investing in your professional growth, opening doors to new opportunities, and solidifying your reputation as a respected and sought-after professional in your industry.

6. Unleashing Innovation: Fueling Tomorrow's Success

Innovation is the lifeblood of progress, propelling industries forward and reshaping the way we live and work. It's the force that disrupts traditional norms, introduces novel solutions, and creates pathways to unprecedented achievements. In today's rapidly evolving landscape, the importance of innovation cannot be overstated. It is the driving force behind competitive advantage, market relevance, and sustainable growth for individuals and organizations alike.

Igniting Progress

To build and enhance innovation, fostering a culture that encourages and nurtures these traits is paramount. Start by cultivating an environment where diverse perspectives are embraced and ideas are welcomed, regardless of hierarchy or origin. Encourage open communication and brainstorming sessions that inspire free-flowing ideas. Collaboration is essential; leverage the power of cross-functional teams to tap into different expertise and viewpoints, sparking fresh insights and solutions.

Continuous learning is a cornerstone of innovation. In addition to skill development covered earlier, experimentation is crucial; embrace a willingness to try new approaches and learn from both successes and failures.

Allocate dedicated time for creative exploration. Incorporate designated periods for employees to work on passion projects or innovative ideas outside their usual responsibilities. This "innovation time" nurtures intrinsic motivation and allows individuals to channel their creativity into tangible outcomes. I usually dedicate Friday afternoons to fresh ideas and continuous learning, and I urge my team to embrace this practice.

Invest in fostering a growth mindset where challenges are viewed as opportunities and failures are seen as stepping stones to improvement. Managers, recognize and celebrate innovation, showcasing successful initiatives and the individuals behind them. By promoting a culture that values creativity and innovation, you empower individuals to think beyond the norm, solve complex problems, and contribute to the evolution of your field.

Innovation isn't a one-time effort; it's an ongoing commitment to pushing boundaries, embracing change, and envisioning new possibilities. By building a culture that prioritizes creativity, encourages exploration, and celebrates innovation, you position yourself, your team, and your organization to lead the charge in shaping the future.

7. Fostering Self-Confidence: Believing in Your Capabilities

Often, the greatest battles we fight are with ourselves—against our doubts, fears, and insecurities. In these battles, our greatest ally is self-confidence. This is the magic ingredient. You need to understand yourself, build confidence, and sustain it through your journey of success, even when the odds seem stacked against you.

Believing in Oneself

Self-confidence is about having faith in your capabilities to undertake unknown challenges. You don't need to hold all the answers; instead, know where and how to uncover solutions, even on uncharted paths. Consider Steve—he likely didn't possess immediate answers, but he embraced his ability to learn, adapt, and conquer.

The Muscle of Self-Confidence

Much like a muscle growing mightier through exercise, self-confidence becomes stronger the more you use it. Confidence propels us to take the first step, and each subsequent step fortifies it further. Just as a bird takes its maiden flight with faith in its wings, we must launch into our journeys with unwavering belief in our capabilities.

Facing the Mirror Image

Building self-confidence begins with self-acceptance—recognizing your strengths and vulnerabilities. It doesn't entail complacency, but rather, navigating waters with a clear grasp of your abilities. Self-acceptance involves giving your best by having the confidence that your best suffices for both your role and aspirations. Maintaining a wholesome rapport with your mirror image—your true self—is pivotal.

The Boldness to Seek Assistance

Elevating self-confidence entails the courage to seek guidance and answers when needed. Especially for managers, acknowledging knowledge gaps and inviting inputs from the team members are absolute signs of strength. Reach out to mentors, peers, and industry experts as required. Utilize every resource at your disposal to navigate complexities.

In essence, self-confidence serves as the "magic" ingredient for enduring transformation and evolution. It's the cornerstone of adaptability, resilience, and tenacity. While the journey to cultivate these traits may pose challenges, self-confidence helps us traverse it not with trepidation, but with unwavering optimism.

Financial Management: Building Your Own Safety Net

Can you imagine the whirlwind of "what-ifs" our minds whip up? *What if I lose my job and never get another job? What if my bank tanks like Silicon Valley Bank did? What if my stock investments go belly up?* Sounds familiar, right?

When the acquisition was announced in my company, the first concern I heard from many of my team members was about their ability to manage their responsibilities without the salary if they lost their jobs.

I may not be a certified financial advisor, but I can't ignore the elephant in the room—the fear of financial instability, especially when we face the prospect of a job loss.

These fears, while normal, can sometimes run wild, painting a picture that's far more catastrophic than reality typically dictates. The key is not to let these hypothetical worries take the driver's seat.

Instead, focus on the practical, more probable scenarios we might encounter.

Remember, our fundamental needs are not extravagantly expensive, and they can be met even in times of hardship. In case of a job loss, keep in mind that this situation, as challenging as it may be, is temporary. You've got tools and resilience. Understand financial management matters—beyond job insecurity, it's about fostering long-term financial health and independence. Budgeting, saving, investing, and income diversification are essential tools to navigate any professional or personal hurdle.

- **Stashing Away for Rainy Days**

  "Save for a rainy day" isn't just old advice. Start saving from early in your career. Living within your means is vital, too. Tech jobs are indeed unpredictable, so, having an emergency fund equivalent to three to 12 months of basic expenses can be a lifeline. This cushion eases job search stress or career exploration.

- **Be the Boss of Your Money**

  Try to manage your spending within 70% of your take-home income monthly. Debt sure causes a significant burden and is a stress factor. So, try to keep it minimal. Keep your credit card bills really short term, not more than one to three months. Financial health equals mental well-being, aiding job uncertainty management

  Planning a career shift or entrepreneurship? Save more and keep an additional buffer for training or initial start-up costs and be disciplined with your spending limits.

- **Discover New Money Trails**

  Good financial management isn't just about saving and budgeting. It's also about finding new streams of income. Part-time gigs, freelancing, or investing can offer cushions during instability. They also open doors to new interests and career prospects.

In a nutshell, think of financial management as your superpower. It empowers you to face job insecurity, maneuver with resilience, and thrive in the evolving job market.

Surfing the Waves of Job Insecurity: Mastering Job Searches and Acing Interviews

So, you've been hit with job insecurity for some reason. Hey, join the club. It's a rite of passage in this fast-paced tech world, and trust me, you're not alone. But there is a surfboard in the choppy career waters—mastering job searches and interview techniques.

- **Stay Ahead of the Game**

  Think of the job market as an ever-changing dance floor. To keep pace, you need to be in sync with the rhythm—know the trends, the hot skills, the employer's wish list. When you have your finger on the pulse of the industry, job insecurity feels less like a ticking time bomb and more like a catalyst for growth.

- **Confidence is Your Superpower**

  And here comes the game changer—confidence. Believe it or not, nailing job interviews is less about perfection and more about self-assurance. It's about walking into that room (or Zoom call), looking your interviewer in the eye, and communicating your worth. Remember, confidence isn't about having all the answers; it's about being comfortable with the questions. It's this very quality that will help you face job insecurity with a level head.

- **Craft Your Career Path**

  Job searching isn't just about landing the next gig. It's a strategic tool for carving your career path. Identify your career goals and work out a plan to get there. Anticipate obstacles, like job insecurity, and equip yourself with strategies to overcome them. You're the architect of your career. Don't let job insecurity shake your foundation.

- **Unleash Opportunities**

  Lastly, acing your job search and interview techniques can unlock doors you never thought you'd open. It might lead you to new roles, new industries, or even an unexpected career shift. Think of job insecurity as a detour, not a dead end. Who knows? It might lead you to a much more fulfilling path.

Now, let's get practical. How do you master job searches and interview techniques?

When job hunting, pinpoint your targets—roles, industries, companies. Tailor your resume for each job application. Harness the power of social media and networking for leads and industry insights. Remember, patience and persistence are the keys to the kingdom.

As for acing interviews, do your homework on the company, the interviewer, and the role, think of potential interview questions, be ready to demonstrate why you're the best fit for the role, but more importantly, be ready to ask questions. Treat it as a two-way conversation—ask questions to see if the company fits your aspirations. Many people miss this point. I have come across many interviewees who, when asked if there are any questions, will say, "Not really." But that can't be true. If not about the company, I am sure you can be genuinely intrigued about the interviewer's experience and career path. Take the opportunity to establish a connection with the interviewer.

Get What You Deserve: The Art of Negotiation

While it may be the final step in the interview journey, negotiation is arguably the most pivotal one. Having showcased your alignment with the role and the value you bring, the negotiation phase becomes your platform to assert your worth confidently. Don't underestimate its significance; it's where you translate your value into tangible terms.

Negotiation is indeed an art—a skillful interplay of assertion and compromise. Here's your guide to mastering this critical phase with finesse.

- **Leverage Your Value Boldly**

  Remember, your negotiation stance should reflect the worth you've demonstrated throughout the process. Don't shy away from asserting the value you bring to the table. Boldly articulate your contributions and how they align with the organization's goals.

- **Strike a Balance**

  Negotiation thrives on balance. While advocating for what you deserve, be open to discussion and compromise. Flexibility in finding mutually beneficial terms showcases your collaborative spirit.

- **Preparation is Key**

  Before entering negotiations, conduct thorough research on industry standards, job market conditions, and the company's compensation practices. Websites such as Glassdoor or PayScale can provide valuable insights. Armed with this knowledge, you can negotiate from an informed standpoint.

- **Communicate with Confidence**

  Clear communication is paramount. Present your points confidently, ensuring you address not just the financial aspect but also other benefits and growth opportunities. Practice active listening during the negotiation process. Again, **respond** to the employer's offer, **don't react**. Take your time, understand the offer, and then articulate your counteroffer, if necessary

- **Be Patient and Professional**

  Negotiations may take time. Maintain professionalism throughout the process, exhibiting patience and understanding. Remember, this phase is an opportunity to build a positive and respectful relationship with your potential employer.

In Summation

In the art of negotiation, you're the orchestrator of your destiny. Embrace it with poise, assert your value, and strike a balance between confidence and collaboration. This final step can be the decisive factor in forging a mutually beneficial partnership that aligns with your aspirations and the company's goals.

Consider this:

> **Love your job but don't love your company, because you may not know when your company stops loving you.**
>
> **—Dr Abdul Kalam**

With these insights, the traditional VUCA paradigm—characterized by volatility, uncertainty, complexity, and ambiguity—can undergo a positive transformation. Instead of viewing challenges through a lens of ambiguity, we can shift our perspective to be **aspirational**, setting forth clear visions, dreams, and accelerated growth targets, even in murky waters. Complexity, with its intertwined systems and processes, can be embraced as a canvas for **creativity**, allowing innovative solutions to emerge from intricate scenarios. In the face of uncertainty, an **upbeat** attitude and the latest trends can drive us forward, focusing on potential opportunities rather than potential threats. And finally, rather than dreading volatility, we can summon **valent**, courageously navigating change and embracing it as a catalyst for growth. By reframing VUCA, we empower ourselves and our organizations to thrive amidst challenges by adopting a more optimistic and proactive mindset.

Navigating the unpredictable terrain of job insecurities demands a multifaceted tool kit beyond the obvious, including flexibility, a thirst for continuous learning, and a knack for networking open doors in unexpected places. Cultivating emotional intelligence fosters the ability to read shifting dynamics and respond thoughtfully. Creative problem-solving and a knack for innovation help you carve niches in changing landscapes. Embracing a global perspective and cross-cultural competence opens avenues beyond borders. Additionally, honing negotiation skills and maintaining a personal brand bolster your position in any scenario. Ultimately, the fusion of these qualities with an unshakable self-belief forms an armor of resilience that transforms uncertainties into stepping stones to greatness.

In life's unpredictable tapestry, in addition to job insecurity, other unexpected threads test our strength—momentary stressors. Join us in Chapter 4 as we unravel some of the common transient challenges and powerful coping mechanisms tailored for instant relief and long-term growth.

Chapter Summary

- Recognize job insecurity as a temporary storm rather than a permanent obstacle.
- Job insecurity is a significant factor in heightened anxiety, depression, and overall well-being decline.
- There are seven different aspects to handling job insecurity: adaptability, continuous learning, networking, emotional intelligence, innovation, and personal brand, all of these underpinned by one MAGIC ingredient—self-confidence.
- Cultivating emotional intelligence is extremely crucial as the repercussions can be significant if not demonstrated well, especially in high-stakes situations.
- Self-belief is indeed the MAGIC ingredient. Understand yourself. Build and sustain confidence through your journey of success, even during the most complex situations.
- DON'T REACT to any situation; take a moment and RESPOND calmly.
- Cultivate savvy financial habits to build a security buffer against job insecurity.
- Negotiation, the final step in the interview process, can be the decisive factor in forging a mutually beneficial partnership that aligns with your aspirations and the company's goals.
- The VUCA world not only creates challenges, but it provides tremendous opportunities.

Traditional VUCA	Reframed VUCA
Volatile	**V**alent
Uncertain	**U**pbeat
Complex	**C**reative
Ambiguous	**A**spirational

Chapter 4

Riding the Ripples: Unraveling Momentary Stressors in the Modern Workplace

In the dynamic and fast-paced world of work, employees often encounter a myriad of momentary stressors that can send ripples through their daily lives. **While these stressors are typically short-lived and not persistent, their effects can be profound.** From high-stakes presentations to the pressure of meeting sales quotas, these fleeting challenges can have a significant impact on mental well-being and overall job performance.

As we delve into specific momentary stressors ahead, it's worth noting a common thread that weaves through their effective management: **Emotional Intelligence**. This aspect was briefly touched upon in the previous chapter. However, as we confront these fleeting stressors, the significance of emotional management takes center stage. While these stressors aren't a constant, the few critical moments they arise demand a deft handling of emotions.

These instances won't always give you ample time to think and prepare, but how you navigate and regulate your emotions within those crucial moments holds substantial repercussions. The fallout can be considerable—impacting your reputation and relationships with colleagues, customers, and investors. A few minutes of mismanaged emotional responses can lead to a sharp decline in trust and goodwill.

Here's a golden nugget of advice: Cultivate the ability to maintain your composure. The key lies in restraint. **Refrain from immediate reactions, especially when negative emotions surge. Regardless of the complexity of the situation, seize a moment to regain your poise, then respond with equanimity.** This practice isn't merely a skill; it's a strategic tool that safeguards your relationships, preserves your brand, and cultivates resilience in the face of rapid stressors.

Conquering the High-Stakes Presentations

High-stakes tech presentations are critical moments where professionals are required to showcase their expertise and ideas to various stakeholders. Such presentations can evoke anxiety, stress, and immense pressure due to the significance of the events. The potential for glory and recognition is enormous if the presentation goes well but so is the risk of disappointment.

One source of stress emanates from the anxiety preceding keynote addresses as they are delivered at prominent conferences or events where industry leaders and experts gather. The fear of speaking in front of a large audience, combined with the desire to deliver a compelling and impactful presentation, can lead to heightened anxiety levels. The pressure to engage the audience and convey complex technical concepts effectively can be overwhelming, impacting the presenter's confidence and mental equilibrium.

Product launches are another nerve-racking affair, which are pivotal moments in introducing new products or services to the market. The preparation, coordination, and anticipation of the product's reception can contribute to stress and anxiety. A successful product launch can lead to significant business growth and recognition while a poorly executed one can have adverse consequences, making the pressure to deliver flawlessly intense.

Another high-stress scenario is during investor pitch sessions, where the future of a tech venture hangs in the balance from potential investors. These pitches are crucial for securing financial support and gaining credibility for the business. The pressure to showcase the company's value proposition, financial projections, and growth potential can cause stress and anxiety among presenters. The fear of rejection and the impact on the company's future can further exacerbate the mental burden.

Coping with the stress of high-stakes tech presentations requires a combination of preparation, resilience, and more importantly, self-confidence.

First and foremost, don't think about you. Think about what's in it for the audience from your presentation. Even in investor pitches, it's not just about how good your product is but about why the investor should be interested and what the uptake is for them. With this, the focus shifts from yourself to the audience.

Next, rigorous preparation and practice are non-negotiable. Originality of content and a thorough understanding of the subject matter are paramount. Crafting unique and authentic content not only captures the audience's attention but also showcases your expertise. This ensures confidence and fluency, enabling you to engage with the audience on a deeper level. Rehearsing the presentation bolsters confidence, curtails anxiety, and heightens performance.

Above all, believe in yourself. You are the presenter due to your proficiency. Refrain from dwelling on potential negative outcomes during preparation; it's a prime source of anticipatory stress.

If, despite solid preparation, you are still nervous or anxious about the presentation, remember that you are not alone, Sweaty palms, a quivering voice, or momentary lapses are part of a shared and common experience. Combat these by experimenting with relaxation techniques, like a few minutes of deep breathing or quick meditation, quelling anxiety before the spotlight. Adopt practical pre-presentation rituals, such as calming deep breaths accompanied by self-assurance affirmations. For example, take ten deep breaths in and exhale through the mouth and say to yourself, "I am going to ace this presentation" just before your turn to speak. Greeting the audience or a quick equipment check can provide a buffer to gather your composure before you begin the topic.

Record and analyze your presentation to continually refine your approach. Anticipate advancements like AI-powered virtual assistants that provide voice and video analysis, offering tailored improvement suggestions. By embracing these strategies and cultivating unwavering self-belief, you'll be poised to navigate the tempestuous waters of high-stakes presentations with finesse and confidence.

Thriving Amidst Software Development Deadline Pressures

In the fast-paced realm of software development, meeting deadlines can be a high-stress endeavor, with tech professionals navigating a maze of challenges.

In rapid development environments or short agile sprints of one to two weeks, such as start-ups or companies focused on continuous deployment, the pressure to deliver the committed features on time can reach its fast-paced settings. The demand for quick iterations and constant adaptation leaves developers little room to catch their breath. The relentless pace can lead to burnout and an overwhelming sense of pressure to produce results within tight time frames. Developers may find themselves grappling with stress and anxiety as they strive to keep up with the rapid development pace while maintaining the quality of their work.

The cornerstone of effectively managing deadline-related stress lies in task prioritization. Identifying business-critical features and functionalities that require timely delivery allows for focused efforts, reducing the burden of multitasking and fostering a clearer path to meeting objectives. This strategic alignment empowers developers to allocate their time with precision and mitigate the sensation of being inundated.

Successful delivery of essential features frequently necessitates cross-functional collaboration. Establishing a pod culture that facilitates seamless collaboration, irrespective of organizational design, proves paramount. By fostering open communication and distributing workloads among pod members, the collective responsibility for meeting deadlines gains prominence, all while expediting the creation of business value.

Additionally, developers should strive to maintain a focus on quality over quantity. Resisting the urge to take shortcuts to meet deadlines can help avoid technical debt and the need for extensive bug-fixing efforts later. Prioritizing quality code contributes to a more sustainable and less stressful development process.

Navigating Service Level Agreements by Tech Support Teams

Navigating the complexities of tech service level agreements (SLAs) is a formidable challenge for IT professionals tasked with adhering to specific performance and resolution timelines. When end-users face significant issues or when ordinary support queries spiral into major customer incidents, the specter of SLA breaches becomes a significant source of stress. The imperative to address these advanced situations both quickly and adeptly can feel daunting. Not meeting SLA standards risks not only financial repercussions but also tarnishes the company's image.

This heightened anticipation from both customers and internal leadership compounds the stress and pressure. Meeting SLA timelines, particularly for intricate issues, where both the company's reputation and customer satisfaction hang in the balance, can heavily tax the mental well-being of IT professionals.

Essential skills in these scenarios include the capability to defuse high-stress situations, engage in effective communication, and employ innovative problem-solving techniques. Keeping a cool head while delving into intricate technical challenges is vital as decision-making as well as problem-solving become more challenging and time-consuming under pressure.

Transparent and timely communication with stakeholders about incident statuses, potential setbacks, and anticipated resolution timelines is pivotal. Often, communication is where things fall through the cracks as tech teams are deeply engaged in resolution efforts. However, stakeholders are generally understanding; after all, SLAs exist for a reason. The key is to keep stakeholders informed, ensuring the updates are both accurate and prompt.

Additionally, organizations can foster a supportive work environment that recognizes the efforts of tech professionals in managing SLAs. Employee recognition and rewards for exceptional performance can boost morale and motivation. Balancing workload and ensuring adequate rest and time off are critical for preventing burnout and promoting mental well-being among tech support teams.

Moreover, fostering a supportive organizational atmosphere is invaluable. Recognizing and rewarding the relentless efforts of IT professionals in upholding SLAs can elevate team morale and drive. Distributing tasks equitably, coupled with ensuring adequate rest and time off, is indispensable in averting burnout and upholding the mental health of the tech support crew.

Targets and Quota Pressures of Sales Teams

In the whirlwind of tech sales, both in business-to-business (B2B) and business-to-consumer (B2C) arenas, sales professionals often find themselves caught in the crosshairs of ambitious targets and stringent quotas. The B2B landscape requires them to unravel intricate and long sales cycles, engage with myriad stakeholders, and negotiate pivotal deals. Meanwhile, B2C representatives race against time, tailoring their pitches to a diverse clientele, keeping pace with rapid product advancements and consistently driving consumer buy-in. The combination of these diverse demands can take a toll on their mental equilibrium.

The pendulum of quarterly and annual quotas only adds to the weight. Living in a performance-driven echo chamber, every quarter and year-end looms large, casting a shadow of daunting targets. The constant tug-of-war between meeting these targets and adapting to the evolving marketplace can induce significant anxiety. This sentiment is magnified by the specter of consecutive underperformance. For instance, the harrowing experience of a sales representative spiraling into a panic attack, fearing back-to-back quota misses, underscores the intense pressures they face.

Yet, amidst these challenges, the key to resilience lies in holistic strategies. Prioritizing a harmonious work-life balance is not just advisable, it's imperative. Furthermore, taking time for self-reflection, celebrating incremental victories, and keeping expectations grounded can serve as a bulwark against burnout. But perhaps, the most pivotal is the art of relationship-building. Engaging with customers authentically, understanding their pain points, and delivering genuine value can be the differentiators. After all, a discerning customer can easily differentiate between value-driven sales and those stemming from sheer desperation, the latter potentially opening the door to skewed negotiations detrimental to both parties. Lastly, embracing challenges as learning curves, rather than impediments, can instill a resilient, growth-centric mindset.

Navigating the Dual Demands of Work and Motherhood

Reentering the workforce post-maternity presents a unique juggling act for mothers. Merging the demands of a profession with the responsibilities and emotional pull of a new baby often serves as a crucible for heightened stress and self-doubt.

The initial days back can feel like an emotional roller coaster. Mothers experience as much separation anxiety as their babies. The heartache of leaving one's child, amplified by challenges like securing trustworthy childcare and navigating breastfeeding logistics at work, takes a toll. To add to the mix, disrupted sleep cycles from caring for an infant can leave mothers feeling perpetually drained, affecting their work efficiency.

Returning to work isn't just about navigating emotional challenges; it's also about embracing a potentially transformed workplace. Mothers returning to their roles may find the technological landscape or the nature of their work has significantly evolved during their absence. This shift demands not just emotional but also professional adaptability. And when you toss in the learning curve associated with new tools, updated processes, or a modified work environment, it can feel like starting a new job altogether.

Open communication becomes even more vital in this scenario. Conversations with employers and colleagues about not only personal challenges but also professional upskilling needs can pave the way for a smoother transition. Many returning mothers might benefit from training sessions, workshops, or simply some buffer time to get acquainted with the new work ecosystem. Embracing flexibility, such as phased work hours or a gradual return, can provide the bandwidth to assimilate these changes without feeling overwhelmed.

Building a strong support network—encompassing family, friends, and understanding peers—can offer guidance, both in managing emotional challenges and navigating the new professional terrain.

But perhaps the most crucial ingredient in this transition recipe is self-compassion. Beyond the emotional and physical toll, professional recalibration demands patience and resilience. It's natural to feel like you're playing catch-up. Letting go of any associated guilt, seeking out necessary resources for re-skilling, and leaning into available support can make the journey less daunting.

Lastly, there's an old saying: "It takes a village to raise a baby." It underscores the importance of collective effort in child-rearing. Often, mothers bear the weight of wanting to handle everything on their own, driven by misplaced guilt of perceived insufficiency. It's essential to shed this burden and to understand that accepting help is neither a sign of weakness nor inadequacy. Embrace the support, let go of the guilt, and understand that everyone benefits when a mother is supported, both at home and in the workplace.

Remember, returning to work post-maternity is not just about picking up where you left off but often about evolving and growing in your role.

Navigating the Terrain of Visa Holders in the Global Tech Industry

In the tech realm, particularly in the US, a significant number of professionals hold visas. While layoffs are universally challenging, visa holders face additional complexities due to their unique circumstances, often impacting their family life significantly.

The mental stress that visa holders experience extends beyond the professional realm. The fear of visa non-renewal and the potential cascading effects of job loss are significant concerns. The uncertainty of securing a new role and transferring your visa or wrapping up your life within a tight time frame if faced with job loss can create overwhelming anxiety. Moreover, the journey towards permanent residency introduces its own set of apprehensions. The notion that job changes during this process might impede progress only amplifies the pressure.

In the face of uncertainty, it's crucial to adopt a realistic perspective. Understand the nuances of your visa status—both the permissible and restrictive aspects. Plan with clarity and foresight, acknowledging potential scenarios if your role becomes redundant.

While there's merit in optimistic planning—like hoping for a swifter path to permanent residency or seamless visa transfers—it's paramount to steer clear of building castles in the air. Overestimating prospects and prematurely committing to substantial investments, such as purchasing a home, can spiral into unanticipated grief. The weight of confronting job redundancies is not just a personal burden; it reverberates through your family. Moreover, over-optimism can pave the way to substantial financial pitfalls, potentially culminating in significant wealth erosion.

Your choice of where to reside is personal, yet from a professional stance, the tech industry is undergoing significant transformation. Roles are no longer confined to headquarters. Innovation, customer-centricity, and leadership positions can be found worldwide. Even I, for instance, have held leadership roles in India for almost a decade now that were traditionally headquarters-based.

Therefore, if your role faces elimination in your visa-holding country and a return to your home country beckons, remember that role quality need not be compromised. Globalization has permeated most roles, erasing the need to assume job quality discrepancies. While specifics vary, the majority of countries offer comparable opportunities. It's a paradigm shift—don't let visa concerns hinder your potential; instead, embrace the evolving global landscape.

Remember, you're not alone. Many have navigated these challenges and emerged stronger. As you balance career aspirations with visa complexities, equip yourself with information, tap into a supportive community, and approach your journey with resilience. Your ability to tackle these intricacies head-on speaks to your determination and potential to excel in the ever-evolving tech industry.

The Emotional Undertow of Organizational Restructure and Downsizing

In the ever-evolving world of tech, employees often find themselves in the eye of organizational storms, from restructuring to the more emotionally charged realm of downsizing. The introduction of new leadership dynamics, team reshuffling, or comprehensive departmental overhauls can leave many grappling with questions about their roles and professional futures.

It's not just these broader reconfigurations that can send pulses racing. A simple, seemingly innocuous message from a manager or a tap on the shoulder from a senior leader saying, "Can I talk to you for a minute?" has taken on a new weight. Instead of anticipating feedback or a casual discussion, the immediate reaction for many is apprehension. *Is there bad news on the horizon? Is my role in jeopardy?* This is a testament to the heightened sense of awareness and tension felt by many in these fast-changing times.

"Survivor guilt" is another emotional undercurrent that runs deep for those who remain post-downsizing. While grappling with the relief of retaining their position, they're simultaneously beset with guilt for their colleagues who weren't as fortunate. This inner turmoil, characterized by thoughts like, *Why was I spared?* can be mentally exhausting.

It's essential to remember during these times that downsizing isn't always a reflection of individual performance. Unless explicitly stated, it's typically about roles and not the people occupying them. Jumping to conclusions about personal worth or competence can be counterproductive. It's the role, not the individual, which is often under scrutiny during these corporate reshuffles. Thus, it's important not to internalize these organizational changes and let them cast doubts over one's self-worth.

The emotional burden isn't exclusively for employees. Managers, the bearers of tough decisions, walk a fine line, holding the dual mantles of company directives and humaneness at conveying the message to their team members, which is a daunting task. These leaders confront the challenges of impacting lives while maintaining an equilibrium between organizational directives and heartfelt empathy.

While the reasons or "whys" for such shifts might remain at a high level or concealed within the boardroom, there's a foundational belief that employees can lean on the trust that senior leadership is acting for the broader organizational benefit. Irrespective of whether downsizing arose from past miscalculations or mistakes, the truth remains that past actions, while debated, cannot be changed. It's essential to internalize this—that, irrespective of the reasons for downsizing, the decisions made are in the best interest of the broader organization and business at that point in time. This can be a foundation for navigating the turbulence.

Strengthening emotional resilience in these phases becomes pivotal. Organizations need to prioritize transparent communication, explain decisions where feasible, and provide resources like counseling for those in need. Fostering open dialogue, where teams can share and vent, is crucial. Equally important is leadership's empathetic stance, recognizing the human element and ensuring a space where concerns are not just voiced but genuinely acknowledged.

A Consultant's Life through Navigating Client Transitions with Finesse

The life of a consultant is often characterized by constant change and adaptation as they move from one client project to another. The momentary stress experienced by consultants during these transitions is not to be underestimated. Rolling off from a client means leaving behind the comfort zone of a familiar environment, established relationships, and a deep understanding of the project's intricacies. As they wrap up their work with one client, consultants may feel a mix of emotions, including a sense of accomplishment, relief, and even a bit of nostalgia.

However, the stress arises when the reality of rolling on to another client sets in. Each new project presents unique challenges, requirements, and expectations that the consultant must quickly grasp and adapt to. There is pressure to quickly establish credibility, build rapport with the new team, and gain a comprehensive understanding of the client's specific needs and goals. The uncertainty surrounding the starting point of a new project can be daunting as consultants must navigate uncharted territory and demonstrate their expertise and value to the client. Despite the stress, this transitional period is also an opportunity for personal and professional growth as consultants learn to be agile and flexible, and continuously improve their skills to provide the best service to each client they encounter.

Dealing with the momentary stress of transitioning between clients as a consultant requires a proactive approach and a positive mindset. Firstly, accepting the nature of the work is crucial; recognizing that change is an inherent part of the consulting profession and can help alleviate some of the anxiety associated with rolling off and on to new projects. Embracing the dynamic nature of the job enables consultants to remain open to new challenges and opportunities for growth.

Secondly, mental preparation is key. Before starting with a new client, take some time to mentally prepare yourself for the upcoming challenges. Reflect on the lessons learned from previous stints and approach each new client onboarding as an opportunity to apply that knowledge. Emphasize the value you bring to the table and be confident in your expertise, which will help build credibility with the new client.

Furthermore, it's essential to think beyond the immediate stress and focus on the long-term benefits of the consulting experience. Each new project offers exposure to diverse industries, challenges, and perspectives, contributing to a broader skill set and a more well-rounded professional profile. Embrace the chance to expand your horizons and gain invaluable experience that can propel your career forward.

Managing Unpredictable Technical Glitches

Picture this: You're deep into a critical conversation, and suddenly, the call drops. Your video freezes at the most inopportune moment, or worse, a sudden power outage leaves you in darkness. Maybe you're racing against the clock to reach a face-to-face meeting, but traffic has other plans, transforming your timely arrival into a late entrance. While we'd love for technology and logistics to be seamless, life has its share of unpredictable glitches that can escalate stress levels in an instant.

It's important to remember that in our digitally intertwined age, almost everyone has experienced a call drop, audio cut-off, or some other technical hiccup at some crucial juncture. While these moments can be immensely frustrating, they're also widely understood and empathized with. Most industry professionals recognize the unpredictable nature of these glitches. As the saying goes, "Don't sweat the small stuff."

Acceptance is a powerful tool. The first step to riding the waves of technical turbulence is acknowledging what's out of your grasp. There's no merit in getting flustered over glitches you can't control. Instead, a proactive approach can transform potential stressors into mere bumps on the digital highway.

For instance, if you're aware of your area's penchant for power glitches, having backup power on standby is prudent. And if bandwidth woes are a frequent companion, a heads-up to your team about potential video limitations can manage expectations effectively. On the logistical side, if you've got a crucial face-to-face meeting, factoring in a time buffer can be a game changer, cushioning the blow of unexpected delays.

Open and prompt communication remains your best ally when disruptions occur. A candid admission like, "I'm having some connection issues" can defuse tension and foster understanding. In moments where plan A goes awry, flexibility becomes your superpower. Being late because of traffic? Dial into that meeting. Low on bandwidth? Switching to audio-only can save the day.

Lastly, remember the beauty of imperfection. Digital disruptions don't undermine your professionalism or passion. With adaptability and a proactive mindset, you can smoothly sail through most tech tides. So, when the inevitable glitch pops up, breathe, recalibrate, and remember we're all navigating these digital waves together.

Insights and Impacts of Tech Performance Reviews

Performance evaluations in the tech world can trigger a mix of emotions among employees as they anticipate annual reviews and feedback. Tech professionals pour their heart and soul into their roles, and invest considerable effort throughout the year, making the annual review an eagerly awaited moment of reckoning. The suspense of these assessments, holding sway over career trajectories, can oscillate employees between stress and hope. Employees may grapple with self-doubt and fear of potential areas for improvement. On the other hand, positive feedback and recognition can boost morale and motivation, reinforcing their sense of accomplishment and dedication to their work.

The shadow of performance improvement plans (PIPs) is often perceived with unease. Instituted when performance doesn't hit the mark, PIPs can set off alarm bells, amplifying anxiety. The daunting journey from underperformance to proving one's mettle is mentally taxing. But every cloud has a silver lining. PIPs, if approached positively, can pivot from a challenge to a catalyst, driving individuals to sharpen their skill set and emerge stronger. Channeling a growth-centric outlook and tapping into the wisdom of mentors can reshape the PIP narrative from a hurdle to a growth leap.

For managers, review season is a tightrope walk. Crafting candid yet uplifting feedback, they grapple with the dual responsibility of maintaining organizational standards while bolstering team spirit. PIPs further complicate this balance. As they guide struggling team members, managers juggle the subtleties of communication, striving for a blend of empathy and encouragement without compromising on results. Balancing these dynamics, all while ensuring fairness and alignment with the company's vision, is indeed a monumental task, shedding light on the multifaceted challenges managers face.

In summary, it's evident that in today's fast-paced and competitive work environments, individuals often encounter momentary stressors that can significantly impact their performance and well-being. Fortunately, the advent of virtual AI assistants has opened new possibilities for supporting employees during these crucial moments. By leveraging cutting-edge technology, AI assistants can provide practical guidance to individuals just before or in real time during key stress-causing events. For instance, through the analysis of voice and video during presentations, these intelligent assistants can identify signs of nervousness, lack of confidence, or other potential stumbling blocks. Subsequently, they offer personalized tips and strategies to improve delivery, body language, and communication skills, empowering employees to handle stressful situations more effectively and enhancing their overall performance and well-being in the workplace.

In recent chapters, we delved into the challenges of workload stress, job insecurity, and transient stressors, along with their coping strategies. Now, let's pivot to Chapter 5, where we'll explore how these factors impact productivity, marrying technological advancements with the vital human touch.

Chapter Summary

Momentary Stressors	Coping Mechanisms
High-stakes presentations	• Preparation and rehearsal of solid content is important. • Practice mindfulness just before the presentation. • Leverage AI assistance for analyzing presentations and providing suggestions to improve wherever possible.
Software development deadlines	• Prioritize the critical features. • Collaborate with cross-team members with a pod mindset. • Don't compromise on quality over schedule.
Handling SLAs	• Equal and adequate distribution of work. • Timely and transparent comms to stakeholders. • Plan on sufficient rest and downtime.
Sales targets and quotas	• Continuously monitor the progress of targets. • Focus on customer value creation in any situation. • Build long-term client relationships.
Mothers returning to work	• Don't be hard on yourself; take it easy and slow. • Be ready to reskill or adjust to newer ways of working. • Seek and accept help.
Visa holders	• Stay informed of visa regulations and changes. • Be prepared mentally, emotionally, and financially for any possible eventualities. • Don't assume any potential compromises on the role if there is a need to get back to your home country.

Momentary Stressors	Coping Mechanisms
Organizational restructuring and downsizing	• Trust leadership decisions. • Do not take organizations decisions personally. • Focus on the future, not the past.
Consultant's life	• Embrace the nature of the consulting role. • Mental preparation, reflection, and relaxation before/after a client engagement. • Focus on long-term value through diverse assignments.
Technical glitches	• Accept the glitches; anticipate and have a contingency plan. • Stay calm and communicate. • Don't personalize glitches.
Performance reviews	• Stay proactive with self-evaluation. • Embrace a growth mindset. • Seek support and mentoring.

Chapter 5

Thrive Amidst Turbulances: Navigating the Crossroads of Productivity in a Digital Powerhouse

The future of work is here, gleaming with digital sophistication. We're living the prophecy of speculative fiction: artificial intelligence, machine learning, hyper-speed collaborations, completely automated and zero-touch DevSecOps processes and systems, advanced multi-cloud infrastructure, Edge, and beyond. With all these advancements, employee efficiency, ideally, should be at an all-time high. Isn't it baffling that despite all these advanced technologies that make our jobs a lot quicker and easier, we're struggling to keep up with productivity goals and still battling inefficiency? When all seems utopian, why is this so?

The pieces of the puzzle don't seem to fit fully together. Let's explore what is really missing in this productivity equation.

The Silent Productivity Killer: An Unexpected Culprit

With a dramatic flourish, let's set the stage. Picture a room buzzing with the clatter of keyboards, the low hum of servers, brilliant minds across the globe collaborating in real time, pulling needed data and focusing on solving complex business problems, all engaged in bringing technology to life. On the surface, it's a hive of efficiency, each cog turning in harmony with the next, each team member a link in the mighty chain of production.

Beyond the hard drives, routers, and screens, there's a silent force at play, capable of grinding this potential super-effective machine to a halt, draining productivity and sapping efficiency. It's not faulty hardware, nor a software bug or network glitch. It's not even the well-documented challenges of global collaboration or the growing complexities of managing a multicultural, multigenerational workforce.

It's something far more personal, more pervasive, and often more difficult to detect: the mental health of the people who power the technology. The **true intellectual property** of our industry. Yes, you read that right. Not the gigabytes, not the processors, not the state-of-the-art collaboration tools, or cutting-edge AI but the human mind itself.

As mentioned in Chapter 1, as per the **WHO:**

> **Globally, an estimated 12 billion working days are lost every year to depression and anxiety at a cost of US$ 1 trillion per year in lost productivity.**

These staggering figures aren't just numbers on a balance sheet. They're signposts pointing to a vast, often overlooked issue that has profound implications for how we understand productivity in our hyper-connected, advanced, tech-driven era.

Surprised? Well, you're not alone.

The truth is, despite our quantum leaps in technological advancement, we're still human. We're wired for connection, we need balance, and we're affected by our mental and emotional states. Our productivity is not just about how efficiently we can operate a software program or how quickly we can troubleshoot a hardware problem. It's also about how well we can manage stress, foster resilience, maintain a positive mindset, and stay happy. Let's take a deep dive into this lesser-known, but significantly impactful, side of the tech-driven workplace.

Consider this:

Source: The WHO. A study conducted by the University of Oxford's Saïd Business School

The Overlooked Connection: Mental Health and Productivity

In the tech industry, we've been so focused on driving technological transformation that we may have overlooked the profound impact this has on our workforce's mental health. In our pursuit of progress, we may have failed to fully understand and address the mental strain that our employees bear. It's a classic case of missing the forest for the trees.

To put things into perspective, consider this staggering statistic:

84% of US workers experienced at least one mental health challenge last year.

This isn't a mere bump in the road; it's a massive crater in our path to productivity.

Depression, anxiety, and other mental health issues can significantly decrease productivity. An employee grappling with these issues may struggle to maintain focus, make decisions, and collaborate effectively with their colleagues. The repercussions can ripple through every aspect of their work life—they might need more time off, their creativity may wane, their overall performance may drop, and they may even need some level of personal daily coping plans. In short, when mental health is compromised, productivity inevitably follows suit.

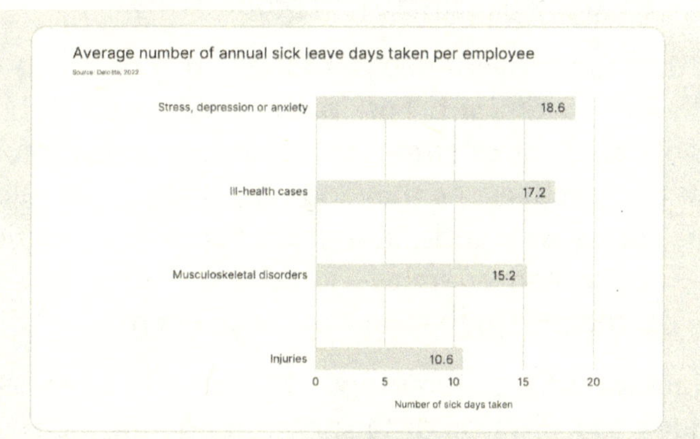

Therefore, as we leverage technological advances to drive efficiency and productivity, we must be mindful of the potential adverse effects they can have on mental health. The pressure to adapt to novel technologies, coupled with the urgency of delivering swift results, can fuel stress and anxiety. The "Great Resignation," a trend of employees opting to leave their jobs in search of better work-life balance and improved mental health, attests to this reality. It is a wake-up call for industries worldwide, underscoring the critical interplay of mental health and productivity.

In essence, as we stand at the crossroads of a tech-driven future, we can no longer afford to ignore the elephant in the room—mental health. The well-being of our workforce isn't a peripheral concern; it's central to our productivity. It's the missing piece of the puzzle, the component we need to prioritize to realize our productivity potential fully.

The Invisible Enemies: Loneliness, Stress, and Changing Life Perspectives

Our world has been shaken to its core by the COVID-19 global pandemic. Employees witnessed loved ones pass away; they took care of elderly family members or kids with special needs while juggling their professional responsibilities. All of this, while working from home, blurring the line between personal and professional life. That's a heavy load to bear, don't you think? Surely, we can't ignore these harsh realities while discussing productivity.

Living through a pandemic has taught us one thing for sure—life can change overnight. For many employees, it brought an unimaginable amount of stress, personal loss, and profound shifts in their life perspectives. As they log into their workstation, they're not just grappling with code, systems, or customer queries. They're wrestling with unseen enemies—loneliness, stress, and a radically altered life perspective in the wake of the pandemic.

The dramatic shift to remote work, meant to keep us safe, had its downsides, too. Physical distancing turned into social distancing, leading to a startling rise in feelings of loneliness among employees. While previously, a watercooler chat or a coffee break could alleviate stress, now it's just them and their screen. The impact? Increased feelings of disconnection, leading to reduced engagement and productivity.

Meet Emily, an employee based in a remote location. Once a busy mother, Emily's twins recently left for college, leaving her in an unusually quiet home. Now, she faces the reality of empty nest syndrome, dealing with overwhelming loneliness. The solitude was more than a physical state; it seeped into her psyche, leading to depressive feelings.

These emotions bled into Emily's work. Previously known as an excellent team player, her productivity started slipping. Emily's story underlines a critical reality: the profound influence our personal lives have on our work performance. Her tale also spotlights the emotional toll remote working can take on an individual, highlighting the need for meaningful human interaction, no matter how advanced our technology becomes.

Then there's the significant strain of losing loved ones or the anxiety of caring for those at high risk. This emotional burden doesn't just disappear when they clock in. It shadows their every step, their every decision, and their every interaction. It impacts their mental health, and consequently, their work performance.

In the face of tragedy, the strength of our resolve can waver. I witnessed this firsthand with a team member who experienced an abrupt, heartbreaking loss when his brother unexpectedly passed away. It took him months to grapple with the harsh reality and find his footing again.

In his grief, he sought solace in work, pushing long hours to distract himself from his emotional pain. Yet, each of us grieves differently, and while work served as his distraction, it didn't address the undercurrent of emotional turmoil that he was experiencing.

How can we balance productivity expectations with emotional support in times of personal crisis? His story serves as a stark reminder of the need for workplaces to acknowledge mental health struggles and offer resources to help employees navigate such hardships.

We also need to acknowledge the particular stressors for those employees who've had to assume dual roles during the pandemic. Many have become caregivers and educators alongside their professional responsibilities. The constant juggling and the pressure to perform well in all these roles can take a toll on their mental health.

> *Meet a financial executive on my team who's caught in a relentless tug-of-war between her professional and personal responsibilities. She manages a 100M+ budget by day while providing care for her special-needs child by night, a task that costs her valuable sleep. Relatives question her dual roles, not understanding that her son's costly treatments necessitate her job. Her perfectionism, coupled with stress and sleep deprivation, places a heavy toll on her mental well-being. This story embodies the often-unseen struggle many employees face—juggling evolving life perspectives, increasing stress, and the demands of their jobs. It's a stark reminder that the personal lives of our employees inevitably seep into their professional performance.*

In essence, the new normal has ushered in a wave of hidden battles that our employees fight daily. Battles that may seem personal, but their impact spills over into the professional realm. They erode mental health, sap energy, and yes, dent productivity. It's an invisible enemy, but its effects on our workforce are very real and need our immediate attention.

- A Gallup poll indicated that only a staggering 13% of employees worldwide are engaged at work.

Worldwide, Actively Disengaged Employees Outnumber Engaged Employees by Nearly 2-1

2011-2012 results among employed residents, aged 18 and older, in 142 countries and areas

	2009-2010	2011-2012
Actively disengaged	27%	24%
Not engaged	62%	63%
Engaged	11%	13%

GALLUP

When employees find meaning in what they do, they are not only more engaged but also exhibit higher levels of productivity. For instance, Tesla employees, driven by the vision of sustainable energy, often report a higher sense of purpose despite the demanding environment.

Finally, it's important to discuss the rising concern of "Silent Quitting" in organizations. This phenomenon occurs when an employee emotionally and mentally disengages from their work, resulting in a severe drop in productivity and performance, despite their physical presence in the role. The shift to remote work and the resultant feelings of isolation exacerbated this. Employees may feel overlooked, unappreciated, or disconnected, leading to a silent but substantial impact on overall organizational efficiency. These feelings are often tied to mental health struggles, further highlighting the need to address mental health in the workplace.

The Manager's Dilemma: Balancing Self-Care and Team Productivity

Consider another team member, a manager who juggles professional responsibilities while bearing the emotional weight of his father's Alzheimer's condition. Each call at work sparks a dread that his father has gone missing. This stress is a constant undercurrent to his work day, stretching his ability to focus and deliver. His story exemplifies the reality many managers face—balancing self-care with the pressure to drive team productivity, all while battling personal emotional storms.

Such predicaments emphasize the manager's dilemma in today's complex work environment: maintaining personal well-being, upholding professional standards, and guiding team productivity amidst personal turbulence.

Envision a ship's captain navigating stormy seas, continually adjusting the course. As a manager, you are responsible not only for your well-being but also for the productivity and mental health of your diverse, geographically dispersed team. The challenge isn't just about hitting project targets; it's about ensuring team members' mental health in the process.

This twofold responsibility can feel like walking a tightrope. However, achieving perfect balance isn't the goal; it's about harmony. As a manager, your task is to harmonize your well-being with that of your team. Self-care isn't selfish; it's a prerequisite to genuinely supporting your team. By prioritizing your mental health, you'll be better equipped to help your team navigate these choppy waters.

Managers, like their team members, grapple with life changes and mental health struggles. Often, they have to reconcile personal emotional health with the responsibility of supporting their team members. In this endeavor, they might feel compelled to maintain a façade of strength, concealing their struggles to preserve their team's morale.

Moreover, managers must understand and empathize with the unique cultural contexts and personal struggles of team members scattered globally. It isn't merely about managing tasks but people, each with distinct backgrounds, cultures, and challenges.

Addressing diverse team needs while maintaining focus on a common goal can be taxing, especially when physical cues and casual check-ins are not feasible. Therefore, managers need to refine their emotional intelligence and promote open communication to genuinely understand their team members' mental health struggles.

As a result of these global shifts, the role of the manager has transformed. It extends beyond driving team productivity and managing projects. It now involves fostering an environment where team members can flourish both personally and professionally despite unprecedented challenges.

In this landscape, where organizations are laying off mid-level managers assuming it is a redundant layer, we need to realize that a good manager's role is continuously evolving and becoming more crucial in driving team productivity.

- **70% of managers believe there are "structural" barriers to providing mental well-being support for their reports.**

- **Only 38% of HR respondents say that their line managers are equipped to have sensitive conversations around mental health.**

  * Source: Spill Guide

How do we address the above? Let's explore it in the following sections.

Empathy in Action: Powering Today's Workspace

Productivity and success must be reimagined beyond traditional notions. The mental well-being of the very people who render our technological achievements possible should take center stage. We must cultivate an empathetic culture that recognizes the impact of mental health on productivity.

The question is: Are we truly acknowledging each other at work? Beyond the exchange of professional pleasantries and collaborative deadlines, are we recognizing the whole person behind the employee badge, the human whose life transcends the confines of work? The call for empathetic workplaces has never echoed louder.

Empathy—the ability to understand and share another's feelings—does not merely mean sympathizing with a colleague's plight or lending a listening ear during tough times. It's a deeper, more active process that involves recognizing, validating, and acting upon the emotional states of those around us.

Even amidst advanced AI, powerful collaboration tools, and streamlined software methodologies, we remain profoundly human, uniquely imperfect, carrying our burdens. Our workplaces, whether a tech firm or a small enterprise, should offer a sanctuary where we can bring our authentic selves, feeling understood and supported.

Workplaces that cultivate empathy create an atmosphere where employees feel seen and understood. This emotional understanding promotes a sense of belonging and encourages open, honest communication. When employees feel heard and understood, they're more likely to contribute their best work, collaborate effectively, and stay engaged.

Furthermore, empathetic leadership plays a crucial role in navigating the intricacies of mental health in the workplace. Leaders who approach their teams with empathy foster an environment of trust and understanding. They are better equipped to recognize signs of mental distress early on and can guide their team members towards the appropriate resources for help. Microsoft CEO Satya Nadella, in his book *Hit Refresh*, places empathy at the heart of his leadership philosophy and argues that it is crucial for innovation and growth.

Visualize a work environment where you're valued as an entire human being, your personal struggles understood, and you're given room to manage them. Empowering, isn't it? This is the transformative power of empathy.

A work culture steeped in empathy does more than promote mental well-being. It enhances morale, fosters camaraderie, and creates a ripple effect of positivity, encouraging everyone to deliver their best, thereby boosting productivity. Empathy should not be a hollow buzzword but a demonstrated action.

In our age of remote work and technological transformation, empathy must not be a peripheral concept; it should be deeply ingrained in our work culture. This means leadership demonstrating empathy, peers encouraged to empathize, and organizational policies embodying this value. It's not just about endorsing mental health but cultivating an environment of belonging, open dialogue, and acceptance.

The days of viewing workplaces as mere spaces for work are behind us. Today, they are communities and support systems that need to be deeply rooted in empathy. As we all navigate unfamiliar territory, empathy is our compass. It's high time we place empathy at the heart of our workplace culture and reevaluate our definition of "productivity."

However, fostering empathy in the workplace is not a passive process. It requires active efforts from everyone within an organization.

This can involve empathy training programs, team-building activities, open forums for discussion, and policies that encourage understanding and inclusivity.

Embracing empathy is more than a feel-good initiative—it's a strategic investment in the mental well-being of employees, and by extension, the overall health of the organization. As the modern workplace continues to evolve, empathy will be instrumental in shaping work cultures where employees can thrive, both professionally and personally.

Looking Ahead: The Role of AI/ML in Mental Health Management

Despite our present challenges, the future need not be bleak. Envision a tech-driven era where artificial intelligence and machine learning platforms monitor and promote employees' mental health daily, directly contributing to productivity enhancements. Imagine managers leveraging these platforms to help their teams excel both in mental health and productivity.

There are already tools like X.ai, an AI personal assistant that schedules meetings. By handing overscheduling to an AI, employees can focus on more meaningful work, reducing the cognitive load and the subsequent stress associated with juggling administrative tasks. Apps like RescueTime analyze your daily habits and help you set specific goals to improve productivity. Or consider mindfulness apps like Headspace or Calm, which encourage mental well-being as a pathway to increased productivity. These apps provide guided meditations and are known to enhance mental fortitude. AI-driven chatbots, such as Woebot, have emerged as virtual mental health allies.

As we advance into the future, it's crucial to not only adapt to emerging challenges but also harness the transformative potential of technology. AI/ML has already brought remarkable changes in various sectors of our lives. However, its proactive application in managing mental health, particularly in the workplace, remains underutilized. Thankfully, this narrative is shifting as we increasingly recognize the benefits AI/ML—especially GenAI—can offer in enhancing **proactive** mental well-being and productivity.

Consider a workplace where AI-based platforms could monitor the mental health of employees in real time. A system where indicators of stress, anxiety, or depression can be recognized early and addressed promptly. Visualize AI chatbots doing mental health screening and offering immediate, personalized support to employees 24/7. A virtual assistant on whom our employees can lean on to seek suggestions/assistance to handle their day-to-day work challenges that are causing stress and anxiety. These scenarios might sound far-fetched, but they are within our reach. AI algorithms can analyze data from various sources to identify patterns and detect early signs of mental health issues. With predictive analytics, it can forecast potential mental health crises, enable early intervention, and completely address the issue before it truly becomes a psychological problem or full-blown crisis.

For managers, these AI-powered platforms could offer data-driven insights into their team's mental health, enabling and coaching sensitive and supportive conversations. For employees, these systems could act as safety nets, providing the necessary tools and resources for effective mental health management. But the key to their success remains an open and accepting workplace culture.

Despite the promise of AI/ML in mental health management, its implementation must be responsible and ethical. Employee privacy and data security are paramount, and systems must ensure confidentiality and transparency about data usage.

When harnessed responsibly, AI/ML can revolutionize mental health management at work, bridging the gap between mental well-being and productivity. Such technology can help build empathetic workplaces that value and nurture mental well-being, consequently boosting productivity, morale, and overall organizational efficiency.

Addressing the Skeptics: Why Investing in Mental Health Makes Business Sense

Let's take a moment to address the elephant in the room. Why should a company invest in mental health? Isn't it a private issue, better handled by individuals themselves? Doesn't it distract from the "real" work at hand? To those who harbor these concerns, we argue that in today's hyper-connected, always-on work environment, the line between personal and professional has blurred more than ever before. Plus, mental health isn't a switch that can be toggled off during working hours. It subtly, yet significantly, influences creativity, decision-making, and collaboration—virtually every facet of productivity. When employees suffer, their work suffers, too, and so does the bottom line of the company. So, isn't it more distracting to ignore this pressing issue, hoping it will resolve on its own? Instead, forward-thinking organizations are realizing the wisdom in addressing mental health proactively, viewing it not as a "distraction" but as an essential part of their holistic approach towards employee well-being, and by extension, sustained business success. Now, more than ever, mental health matters—both at home and in the workplace.

Consider this :

- **More than half (52%) of employees don't feel they get enough support from their employer for their mental well-being.**
- **Initiatives aimed at improving workplace mental health can yield a return of interest up to 800% due to higher productivity, fewer sick days, and lower staff turnover.**
- **Having better mental health initiatives in place can save the UK's businesses up to £8 billion every year.**

  * Source: Spill Guide

Beyond Efficiency: Redefining Tomorrow's Productivity

In the march of technology, we must not leave its creators—us—in the dust. Our definition of productivity must evolve to encompass the mental well-being of our workforce. We must strive for a future where mental health is valued, nurtured, and integral to our technological achievements.

As employees, we must recognize mental health's importance in our personal well-being and professional success. As managers, we should strive to create empathetic and supportive work environments that value mental health and acknowledge its role in fostering productivity.

Organizations need to view mental health not as a peripheral issue but as a fundamental aspect of their business strategy. Doing so can transform workplaces into havens of creativity, innovation, and productivity, free from the restraints of mental health issues.

Below are examples of organizations that have come up with creative ways to focus on mental health.

- **Salesforce: Creating Havens of Calm**

  Salesforce has turned its offices into sanctuaries for mental rejuvenation. One of its most striking initiatives is the inclusion of "Mindfulness Zones" on every floor of its towering skyscrapers. These zones are akin to modern-day monk cells—spaces designed for tranquility and reflection, devoid of technological interruptions.

- **Atlassian: Championing Autonomy and Innovation**

  The software tool company **Atlassian** conducts **quarterly "ShipIt Days"** in which employees may work on anything related to **the company's** products. In those 24 hours, employees put their usual work aside and focus on a project they are passionate about.

This serves multiple purposes. Firstly, it acts as a pressure release valve, allowing employees to take a break from their routine. Secondly, it respects the creative autonomy of the employees, recognizing that they are not just cogs in a machine but individuals with unique perspectives. This sparks innovation, bolsters employee morale, and creates an environment where productivity is driven by passion rather than compulsion.

As we've discussed in previous chapters, whether it's the high-stress environments, the constant hustle, or the looming job insecurity, all these factors invariably affect our mental health, and consequently, our productivity. By understanding and addressing the mental health issues that are spawned from these workplace situations, organizations can redefine their definitions of productivity and success.

As we look ahead, we can envision a future where AI/ML platforms play a pivotal role in managing and promoting mental health in workplaces. By responsibly and ethically integrating these technologies, we can unlock a world of possibilities for healthier, happier, and more productive workplaces.

Navigating productivity in a rapidly evolving digital world necessitates a holistic approach, where mental well-being and empathy lie at the heart of modern workspaces. However, as we move forward into Chapter 6, it becomes evident that the fabric of mental health is intricately woven with cultural threads. While our efforts to integrate AI and tech-driven insights can tailor support, it's the understanding of diverse cultural nuances that will determine its success.

Chapter Summary

- The traditional definitions of productivity and success need to be reconsidered to emphasize the mental well-being of employees in today's workplaces.
- There is a critical need for empathetic workplaces where mental health is prioritized and its impact on productivity is recognized.
- Workplaces should support employees as whole people, acknowledging their unique burdens and human experiences beyond professional duties.
- Empathy in workplaces boosts morale and promotes a strong sense of camaraderie, leading to increased productivity and efficiency.
- In the era of remote work and technological transformations, empathy should be ingrained in work cultures, supported by leadership, encouraged among peers, and embodied in organizational policies.
- The potential of AI/ML in mental health management at workplaces, including monitoring mental health in real time and providing immediate, personalized mental health support, is vast and largely unexplored.
- Skeptics need to understand that investing in mental health initiatives is not only ethically right but also makes strong business sense, with significant returns on investment due to increased productivity, fewer sick days, and lower staff turnover.
- Both employees and managers have a role to play in fostering empathetic workplaces that prioritize mental health and acknowledge its importance in productivity.
- By integrating AI/ML into mental health management responsibly and ethically, organizations can potentially bridge the gap between mental health and productivity, leading to healthier and more productive workplaces.

Chapter 6

Global Shadows: Universal Struggle with Culture and Mental Health Stigma

As the sun rises on a new day, an office in Tokyo begins humming with activity, housing a finance executive facing burnout due to grueling work hours. Meanwhile, a software engineer in Bengaluru works through the night resolving a production issue. Thousands of miles away, an exhausted team in London wraps up a late meeting as dusk settles. Across the ocean, in Silicon Valley, an entrepreneur grapples with the constant pressure to innovate and raise funds, with the fear of failure looming large.

These snapshots of the global work arena hint at a shared human experience, all too common yet rarely spoken of—the struggle with mental health. These experiences aren't restricted by geographical borders or cultural distinctions. They are a universal phenomenon.

As diverse as our workspaces are, so, too, are our mental health narratives significantly shaped by the cultural contexts in which we're embedded.

Crossing Geographical Lines: Cultural Interpretations

Culture plays a profound role in how we understand and interpret mental health. As each culture is unique, so, too, are its conceptions and perceptions of mental well-being and illness. This diversity adds layers of complexity to addressing the mental health challenges of employees, especially within global organizations.

Medical Model Perspective

From the medical model perspective, mental health is typically viewed through the medical model lens. Here, mental health challenges are seen as diagnosable and treatable conditions, akin to physical health concerns. The emphasis is on individual symptoms, experiences, and interventions, often blending medication and therapy. Recently, there's been a push for insurance providers to equate coverage for mental health treatments with that of physical conditions. Though this stance has played a role in reducing stigmatization, it occasionally misses the broader social, economic, and cultural influences on mental well-being. Despite progress, workplace misconceptions persist, with some still deeming individuals with mental health challenges as unstable or unreliable, further warping the true picture.

Holistic Health Perspectives

From the holistic health perspective, mental health is adopting a holistic stance, emphasizing the intricate relationship between mind, body, and spirit. Here, mental health disturbances might be interpreted as internal imbalances, which can be addressed by reinstating harmony through age-old practices and remedies. Additionally, these societies tend to lean towards a collective ethos, where communal views and values profoundly shape an individual's mental well-being. This interconnectedness can sometimes manifest as societal pressure, creating silent barriers to seeking help due to perceived notions of dishonor to the individual or family.

Intersecting Stigmas: Challenges among Diverse Groups

Within the global workplace's vibrant mosaic of cultures, mental health stigma amplifies, particularly among smaller or diverse groups.

According to **PeopleMatters, women are more at risk for mental health issues than men.** Women, balancing professional and personal roles, often grapple with stress, anxiety, and depression, silenced by societal norms that erroneously equate struggle with weakness.

The LGBT+ community experiences "minority stress" due to systemic discrimination, often concealing their mental health challenges to avoid further marginalization.

Meanwhile, millennials, though more vocal about mental health, wrestle with unique pressures like "impostor syndrome," skyrocketing living costs, and a fiercely competitive job market.

The digital age, while providing resources, paradoxically heightens their sense of isolation due to social media's unrealistic expectations. For these groups, the workplace represents a complex intersection of mental health issues and cultural stigmas, complicating the journey towards seeking help and fostering a supportive environment.

The Impact of Cultural Stigma

While each culture has its unique interpretations of mental health, one commonality across cultures is the stigma associated with mental illness. This stigma often stems from misunderstanding or fear, leading to discrimination and reluctance to seek help. It can make mental health issues seem like personal failings rather than health issues, exacerbating the problem.

The disparity is also evident at the higher echelons of the corporate ladder. The modern workplace often glorifies leaders as tireless, unfazed individuals who thrive under pressure. This narrative indirectly cultivates a culture where acknowledging mental health struggles is seen as a sign of weakness.

- A study published in the ***Journal of Business Ethics*** **in 2020** found that **several corporate leaders chose to hide their mental health issues for fear of professional repercussions and negative judgments.**

In summary, understanding these cultural interpretations is crucial for designing inclusive and effective mental health strategies worldwide. It's a reminder that we must consider cultural nuances when addressing mental health, particularly in diverse global workplaces. The challenge lies in creating an environment that respects and accommodates these cultural differences while also encouraging open conversations and support for mental health.

Cultural Barriers: How Stigmas Shape Our Mental Well-Being

In the bustling hub of India, a dedicated professional and single mother grapples with the aftermath of a life-altering divorce. She's shouldering the weight of raising two young children while keeping up with demanding professional responsibilities. The immense pressure is silently chipping away at her mental health, nudging her towards the edge of anxiety, depression, and low self-esteem.

Her struggles, however, remain private. Held back by cultural stigma, she hesitates to even reveal her divorced status at work, fearing judgment and professional repercussions. She worries about being passed over for exciting projects, fearing her colleagues might judge her or think she's not up to the task given her personal circumstances.

She craves support but does not want to seek professional help, more so due to the societal stigma surrounding it. She's worried about her privacy and the potential impact on her social life and her children's lives.

Amid this turmoil, she finds herself wishing for a confidante—a virtual AI assistant. A non-judgmental, completely private entity that could help her navigate her personal and professional challenges, offering the support she desperately needs. This, to her, is more than a wish—it's a lifeline she hopes to grasp.

Consider this: **Time to Change research** shows that **up to 90% of people with mental health problems experience some form of stigma, whether from friends and family, at work, in education, or during treatment.**

Stigma, particularly when it's deeply ingrained in the cultural fabric, presents a formidable barrier to mental health care and open dialogue. When mental health issues are stigmatized, they are often misunderstood, feared, or dismissed, having a profound impact on individuals, communities, and workplaces worldwide.

- **Suffering in Silence**

  The power of cultural stigma lies in its ability to silence. Many people, burdened by the weight of cultural expectations, find it difficult to express their struggles. The fear of being judged, isolated, or misunderstood can be so overpowering that individuals often choose to suffer in silence. They may forego seeking help from anyone, including a professional mental health practitioner, fearing that the associated stigma could outweigh the benefits of therapy or medication.

- **Impact on Treatment and Recovery**

  When cultural stigma deters individuals from acknowledging their struggles or seeking assistance, it directly impacts their journey towards recovery. Early detection and intervention, often key in managing mental health issues, may not occur. The lack of timely treatment can exacerbate the severity of mental health problems and prolong the recovery process.

- **Effects on Self-Identity and Self-Esteem**

  Cultural stigma can infiltrate the self-perceptions of those struggling with mental health issues. They may internalize the negative stereotypes and prejudices, leading to feelings of shame, guilt, and low self-esteem. This so-called "self-stigma" can make it even harder for them to seek help or discuss their issues, perpetuating a cycle of silence and suffering.

- **Pervasive Impact on Society and the Workplace**

  The cultural stigma associated with mental health doesn't only affect individuals; it reverberates throughout the family, society, and workplace. In a culture where mental health is stigmatized, open conversations about mental well-being may be absent in the workplace, denying employees the supportive environment they need.

In conclusion, the cultural stigma surrounding mental health acts as a significant impediment to mental health care. To create an open, understanding, and supportive culture, we must actively challenge and change these stigmatizing attitudes. It starts with fostering a society and workplace where mental health can be discussed without fear of judgment, leading to better awareness, understanding, and ultimately, improved mental well-being.

A Time for Change: The Renewed Role of HR and Leaders

As we dive deeper into the 21st century, it becomes abundantly clear that the time for change is upon us. Mental health, once considered a personal issue shrouded in stigma and silence, has emerged into the limelight, demanding a concerted, collective response. The modern workplace, with its evolving dynamics and pressures, has a pivotal role to play in this transformation.

The shared responsibility for mental health in the modern workplace is not a simple notion; it's a multifaceted concept involving a broad spectrum of stakeholders, from top management to entry-level employees. It's about creating an ecosystem where everyone is equipped to understand, acknowledge, and respond to mental health issues effectively.

In the context of the workplace, collective responsibility begins with leadership. The role of leaders extends beyond setting targets and driving performance. Leaders bear the crucial responsibility of creating a work culture where mental health is acknowledged as integral to overall well-being and productivity. This includes setting the right tone through open conversations about mental health, leading by example, and fostering a culture of empathy.

Next comes the role of human resources and organizational policies. It's here where the rubber meets the road. HR teams must ensure that policies surrounding mental health are comprehensive, compassionate, and communicated clearly to all employees. Policies alone, however, are not sufficient. They must be complemented by resources such as counseling services, flexible work arrangements, and wellness programs that cater to the mental well-being of employees.

The collective responsibility for mental health also trickles down to the team level. Managers and team leads, often the first point of contact when employees face struggles, need to be equipped with the right tools and training to respond effectively. This means not only identifying signs of struggle but also knowing how to guide the individual towards the right resources.

Lastly, but perhaps most importantly, comes the role of individual employees. Everyone in the organization, irrespective of their role or level, shares a part of the responsibility. It's about fostering an environment of understanding and support among peers. Individual responsibility also involves self-care and seeking help when needed, thereby breaking the stigma around mental health one step at a time.

Our collective responsibility for mental health in the modern workplace is not merely a moral obligation, it's a business imperative.

The Power of Empathy: Fueling Positive Change

As the contemporary work environment becomes more complex and demanding, an unexpected protagonist has taken center stage in the narrative of a healthier workplace: empathy. This fundamental human ability, the capacity to understand and share the feelings of others, has proven to be a powerful catalyst for positive change in today's workplaces.

Workplaces that cultivate empathy create an atmosphere where employees feel seen and understood. This emotional understanding promotes a sense of belonging and encourages open, honest communication. When employees feel heard and understood, they're more likely to contribute their best work, collaborate effectively, and stay engaged.

Furthermore, empathetic leadership plays a crucial role in navigating the intricacies of mental health in the workplace. Leaders who approach their teams with empathy foster an environment of trust and understanding. They are better equipped to recognize signs of mental distress early on and can guide their team members towards the appropriate resources for help.

Embracing empathy is more than a feel-good initiative—it's a strategic investment in the mental well-being of employees, and by extension, the overall health of the organization. As the modern workplace continues to evolve, empathy will be instrumental in shaping work cultures where employees can thrive both professionally and personally.

Mental Health Education: Unleashing the Power of Knowledge

Mental health education serves a dual role. Firstly, by providing accurate and clear information about various mental health conditions, their causes, and effective treatments, we can begin to chip away at the misunderstandings that perpetuate stigma. For instance, it's not uncommon for depression to be dismissed as mere sadness, or for anxiety to be minimized as overreacting. Such misinterpretations can lead to a lack of understanding and support, further alienating those struggling with these conditions.

Secondly, mental health education equips individuals with the tools they need to support their own mental well-being and that of their colleagues. This includes recognizing signs of common mental health issues, understanding when and how to seek help, and learning effective coping strategies. For instance, Google's Mental Health First Aid training provides employees with practical skills to support their peers who might be experiencing mental health issues.

Moreover, mental health education encourages self-care and prevention. Just as we understand the role of a balanced diet and regular exercise in maintaining physical health, a similar approach should be taken towards mental health.

However, it's important to note that while education is a critical step, it isn't a standalone solution. For effective mental health support, educational initiatives must be the foundation of a comprehensive approach that includes policy changes, access to virtual AI assistants and/or professional mental health services, and a culture that encourages open conversations about mental health.

Availability of and access to mental health resources can be a game changer. This could include counseling services, employee assistance programs, and mental health days. When employees see that their workplace offers tangible support for mental health, it can go a long way in reducing stigma.

Running anti-stigma campaigns and using testimonials, stories, and data can challenge stereotypes and prejudice around mental health. These campaigns can be tailored to the specific cultural context of the workplace.

Today, mental health is gradually taking center stage in workplace conversations thanks to increasing awareness and advocacy. High-profile executives, influencers, and celebrities in corporate circles are becoming more open about their personal struggles with mental health. Their transparency is critical in challenging entrenched stereotypes and reducing stigma, allowing mental health conversations to emerge from the shadows in boardrooms across the globe. Businesses worldwide are becoming more conscious of mental health, implementing policies like mental health days, supporting work-life balance with flexible schedules, encouraging regular breaks for relaxation and rejuvenation, embracing diversity and inclusion, celebrating cultural events, fostering open dialogues, offering cultural competency training for employees at all levels in addition to comprehensive wellness programs and employee assistance services.

From Strategy to Implementation: Shaping Mental Well-Being-Friendly Workplaces

Transforming mental health strategies into concrete actions requires a comprehensive understanding of successful practices around the world. Various organizations, from multinational corporations to local nonprofits, have implemented innovative measures to foster a mental health-friendly environment. Let's explore these practices, hoping to draw lessons that can guide us in shaping our own mental health strategies.

1. Embedding Mental Health into Company Culture

Unilever

Unilever, a multinational consumer goods company, stands as an exemplar of embedding mental health into its company culture. Recognizing that top-down support is critical, the company's senior leaders have made mental health a strategic priority. Initiatives range from mental health training for line managers, designed to equip them with skills to support their team's mental well-being, to the company's Global Mental Health Ambassadors program, fostering a network of employees who can guide their colleagues to the appropriate resources.

2. Providing Access to Mental Health Resources and Support

Starbucks

Starbucks, a global coffee company, sets a benchmark in providing mental health resources and support to its employees. Realizing the steep costs of professional mental health services, Starbucks offers its US employees and their eligible family members access to 20 free therapy or coaching sessions a year. This investment showcases Starbucks's commitment to providing accessible and substantial mental health support to its workforce.

3. Promoting Work-Life Balance

Basecamp

Basecamp, a Chicago-based software company, places a strong emphasis on promoting work-life balance as a critical aspect of mental health. Measures include a four-day work week during the summer, providing employees with time to recharge, and a policy of no after-hours or weekend work, respecting personal time and preventing burnout.

4. Encouraging Open Conversations about Mental Health

Ernst & Young (EY)

EY, a global professional services firm, has been leading the way in encouraging open conversations about mental health. They launched the "R U OK?" campaign, which encouraged employees to check in with their peers and fostered a culture of care within the organization. This not only normalized discussions about mental health but also strengthened bonds among employees.

5. Localized Employee Assistance Program

IBM

IBM, the multinational technology company, is another example of effectively addressing cultural differences in its mental health initiatives. They've developed localized global mental health programs, such as confidential employee assistance programs and mental health training for managers, ensuring country-specific needs and sensitivities, thereby underlining the importance of culturally informed approaches.

These case studies offer a glimpse of what companies worldwide are doing to create mental health-friendly environments. These measures require significant commitment and investment, but the dividends—in terms of employee well-being and overall organizational health and productivity—are substantial.

We unearthed the pivotal role that cultural understanding plays in not only supporting employees but in breaking barriers that often inhibit mental well-being. As we transition into Chapter 7, our focus shifts to the individual's journey of achieving the delicate equilibrium of work and life integration.

Chapter Summary

- Mental health issues are universal, but their interpretations and stigma can greatly vary across cultures.
- Cultural differences in multicultural workplaces can present unique mental health challenges.
- Promoting open dialogues, providing mental health resources, and incorporating mental health into company culture are successful strategies for managing mental health in workplaces.
- Overcoming cultural stigma in workplaces involves education, leadership support, policy changes, and creating a supportive environment.
- Cultivating an inclusive and understanding workplace culture involves respecting and acknowledging different cultural perspectives on mental health.
- Implementing mental health initiatives that are flexible, adaptable, and culturally sensitive can enhance their effectiveness.
- Several global companies have effectively implemented mental health initiatives by considering cultural differences.

Chapter 7

The Balancing Act: Pursuing Harmony in a World of Work

Throughout my career journey of two decades, one of the most common questions posed to senior leaders is, "How do you achieve work-life balance?" Why is this question so prevalent and important? Why has the same question been asked for decades? And is there a single answer or "secret sauce" to this question? Let's explore.

Work-life balance is said to have come into use in the 1970s/80s as stressed baby boomers strove to achieve a balance between their careers, families, and other areas of their lives, intending to create clear boundaries. Since then, the term is being reevaluated through the shifting generational experiences.

The balance between work and life within the technology industry oftentimes falls heavily towards more work than life, leading to burnout and decreased productivity. In a world where connectivity has no bounds, our lives don't follow conventional boundaries any longer.

Consider this:

> **There is no such thing as work-life balance—it is all life; the balance has to be within you.**
>
> **—Sadhguru, Isha Foundation**

In the current era, work-life balance has become the ability to integrate work and personal life harmoniously, without one taking over another. The traditional interpretation has been replaced by a more dynamic and individualistic concept, with the **balance** differing for each individual based on their personal needs, situations, and circumstances; it's not a one-size-fits-all formula.

Technological advancements have completely reshaped the landscape of work-life balance. Work-life integration thus gains prominence, emphasizing a philosophy that encourages blending personal and professional elements without diminishing the value or enjoyment derived from either.

This concept is less about maintaining balance on a seesaw and more about creating a synergy where professional and personal life mutually enhances each other, creating an ecosystem that nurtures overall well-being.

Consider this:

> **Remember that work and life coexist. Wellness at work follows you home and vice versa. The same goes for when you're not well, fueled, or fulfilled. Work and life aren't opposing forces to balance; they go hand-in-hand and are intertwined as different elements of the same person: you.**
>
> **—Melissa Steginus**

21st Century Challenges: Understanding Obstacles to Achieve Work-Life Balance

Consider this:

> **The challenge of work-life balance is without question one of the most significant struggles faced by modern man.**
>
> **—Stephen Covey**

As the dawn of the 21st century brought about a new era characterized by digital transformation, globalization, and unprecedented pace of change, achieving work-life balance has become an increasingly tough challenge. Understanding the unique obstacles that potentially obstruct the path to this balance is a critical step towards devising effective strategies to navigate them.

- As we described in Chapter 2, a high-velocity competitive environment, "always-on" culture, speed to market, creativity demands, and performance pressure can lead to overwork, burnout, and reduced time for personal activities, thus tipping the balance heavily towards the work side.
- Another challenge lies in societal expectations and pressures. The societal definition of success often leans heavily towards professional achievements, financial stability, and steady career progression. These pressures can inadvertently lead to prioritizing work over personal life, leading to a skewed work-life balance.
- Additionally, the advent of remote work, while providing more control over work schedules, flexibility, and reduction in commute time to the office, has also posed challenges around overwork and isolation and has blurred the lines between professional and personal spheres. Without a designated "workplace," it becomes challenging to create physical boundaries that differentiate work from personal life. This can lead to situations where work bleeds into personal time, thus disrupting the equilibrium.

- Lack of sufficient support from employers is another hurdle employees are facing in their recent quest for work-life integration. Not all organizations prioritize the need for their employees to maintain a balance between their professional and personal lives, like providing options to work from home, flexible work hours, parental leave policies, or mental health management initiatives. Sometimes culture comes in their way. This impacts employees' work-life balance negatively, and thus, their productivity.
- Personal circumstances, such as caregiving responsibilities, single parenthood, or other life-changing events, can demand significant time and emotional energy from employees. Coupled with work demands, these circumstances can pose substantial challenges to achieving balance.

Acknowledging these challenges is the first step to addressing them, and organizations, societies, and individuals must work together to devise strategies that mitigate these issues and promote a healthier, more balanced lifestyle.

The Employer's Role in Work-Life Balance

The tech industry has a historical trend of being supportive of employees' work-life balance needs as much as possible. Although it may not have initially been an employer-led initiative, managers and HR have traditionally responded supportively when employees requested assistance in managing their work-life balance.

My personal experience illustrates this: *When I was returning to work from an eight-week maternity leave in February 2000, I found it extremely challenging to work for eight straight hours in the office while I had to care for an infant at home. I had severely underestimated the energy, effort, and tight schedule required to care for a newborn, and my initial plans were simply not working out. When I told my organization that I could only physically be in the office for four hours/day and needed to work the remaining hours from home in order to nurse the baby on time, my request was accommodated without hesitation. Keep in mind that there was no established concept of "work from home" at that time, and we only had dial-up internet connections! Despite this, as a key designer during that period, I was able to work on design documents from home in the afternoons for a few months.*

What's primarily changing in the present context is the role of employers—in this evolving landscape, they are transitioning from being mere accommodators to active facilitators in the quest for work-life balance.

The Rise of Employer-Led Initiatives: Evolving Policies and Culture

Today's interconnected world has spurred employers to play a pivotal role in reshaping the narrative of work-life balance. Companies now recognize that fostering a healthy work-life synergy not only enhances employee well-being but also drives productivity, creativity, and commitment, which ultimately leads to organizational success.

> **Companies recognize that employees are seeking a more flexible approach to their work schedules. The shift is driven by a recognition that employees who feel supported and able to meet personal needs are more productive, engaged, and committed to their work.**
>
> **—HR Vision**

This understanding has prompted forward-thinking organizations to revisit their policies and culture, striving to create an environment that enables employees to maintain a healthy balance between their personal and professional lives.

The key changes include:

- **Fostering empathy:** Organizations now acknowledge employees' personal lives and commitments and recognize the various pressures they may face. This empathy enables employers to make more informed decisions and formulate policies that cater to the needs of their employees.

- **Flextime and remote work:** Policies like flextime, which enables employees to customize their work schedules, and remote work, which eliminates commuting time, are examples of such changes. These initiatives highlight the idea that productivity isn't about being tied to a desk for a specific number of hours but about delivering quality work regardless of location or time.
- **Family-friendly policies:** These may include generous parental leave, childcare facilities, and policies that allow employees to attend to family emergencies without fear of repercussions. These measures underscore the understanding that employees have commitments beyond work and that supporting these commitments is an investment in the employee's overall well-being, and by extension, their performance and loyalty.
- **Wellness programs:** Employers are initiating custom-tailored programs that promote employee well-being. This may involve access to yoga or mindfulness sessions, onsite fitness centers or subsidized gym memberships, mental health support, and encouragement for employees to pursue hobbies and leisure activities.
- **Culture of respecting personal time:** This means discouraging late-night emails, respecting off days and vacations, and promoting a culture where downtime is seen not as a luxury but as a necessity for rejuvenation.
- **Role model leadership:** Leaders are encouraged to demonstrate healthy work habits, promote open conversations about stress and burnout, have open-door policies, do regular check-ins, and recognize and reward clear outcomes rather than long working hours. Employees often take cues from their leaders, thus leaders who demonstrate this culture set the tone

for the organization's practices and send a strong signal about the organization's commitment to work-life balance.

- **Celebrating the whole person:** Employers are recognizing not only professional accomplishments but also personal milestones, fostering a sense of community and belonging, and reinforcing the importance of life outside of work.
- **Harnessing technology:** Companies are investing in digital tools and practices that promote work-life integration. This includes features like screen time tracking, "do not disturb" modes, and prompts for regular breaks.
- **Measuring impact:** Employers are monitoring employee satisfaction, turnover rates, and productivity levels to gauge the positive impacts of their work-life balance initiatives.

By initiating these changes, employers signal a shift towards a more holistic view of employees, seeing them as individuals with multifaceted lives rather than solely as workers fulfilling professional duties.

Case Studies: Global Organizations Implementing Creative Initiatives

Consider this: As per **Gallup, effective holistic solutions decrease the risk of a worker changing jobs by up to 81%!**

- **Case Study 1: ASANA: Innovative Work-Life Balance Programs**

  Employees are paid to sleep at Asana in one of their "nap rooms," made so employees can rest up, recharge, and de-stress. They offer daily yoga programs and free gym memberships. The in-house culinary team serves three nutritious meals a day using fresh produce from local and organic farms. The company also offers mentor programs that provide free executive coaching, along with monthly workshops with different health-themed focuses, such as a "Debunking Detox" workshop and an immunity workshop before flu season, and on Wednesdays, Asana doesn't hold meetings.

- **Case Study 2: Microsoft: A Holistic Approach to Employee Well-Being**

  Microsoft has introduced a range of flexible working options, such as work-from-home arrangements, flexible hours, and part-time roles. What sets Microsoft apart is its emphasis on health. Not only does the company offer education and resources for smoking cessation, weight management, and fitness training, Microsoft will also fund employees' gym memberships or fitness-related equipment and fitness activity purchases while also providing free Zumba classes, onsite walking and running tracks, along with basketball, volleyball, and baseball courts. Additionally, Microsoft holds "Know Your Numbers" health screening events for their employees and their families. The campus also offers health care services, including onsite clinics, optometrists, and pharmacists. The Microsoft CARES employee assistance program also offers free personal and family counseling, stress management, and referrals for child and elder care. The cafés come stocked with healthy dining options. Microsoft offers onsite grocery and dry cleaning delivery, too!

- **Case Study 3: Intuit: Emphasizing Mindfulness**

  The company's "Fit for Life" program offers meditation and mindfulness classes as reimbursable expenses, as well as incentives for employees engaging in stress-reduction habits, like taking a walk, practicing breathing exercises, or listening to calming music. The company's website provides mindfulness resources, but employees can also find "mindful moment" tips on the whiteboards in the conference rooms.

Navigating Dual Realities: Employee Responsibility

While employers are increasingly initiating measures to aid employees in achieving work-life integration, the responsibility also lies with employees in striking a delicate balance between professional ambitions and personal fulfillment. Both realms offer their own set of demands and rewards. The challenge, then, is to ensure one realm doesn't overshadow the other. This fosters a conducive environment for growth and happiness in both aspects.

Achieving professional success without sacrificing personal fulfillment is not a zero-sum game. However, navigating this path demands careful orchestration, a clear understanding of one's values and goals, and the wisdom to handle inevitable trade-offs. It's a constant negotiation between different facets of life, requiring flexibility and keen self-awareness.

- **Set Clear Goals**

  Achieving this balance often starts with the setting of clear, measurable goals in both professional and personal domains. The key lies in identifying how these goals can harmoniously coexist. For example, if career advancement is a primary professional goal, one must consider the time and commitment it requires. Whereas, if personal goals involve spending quality time with family or pursuing hobbies, the challenge is to accommodate these within the broader framework of professional responsibilities and commitments.

- **Setting Clear Boundaries**

  Once these goals have been identified, it's important to set clear boundaries between work and personal life. One of the best pieces of advice I received from my mom when I had to return to work after my maternity leave and was constantly worried about the baby was, "Give your level best at any moment of the day; don't carry work worries home, and don't take home worries to the office. Focus fully on the task of the moment."

- **Prioritization of Tasks**

  Prioritizing tasks and managing time effectively is crucial. With only 24 hours in a day, effective planning becomes paramount. Begin by identifying your most critical tasks and concentrating your efforts on completing them efficiently. Learn to decline non-essential tasks if they infringe on your personal time. Similarly, make sure to prioritize personal time as well. Schedule personal activities, family time, and hobbies in advance to ensure they're not sidelined.

As **Stephen Covey** wisely said, **"The key is not to prioritize what's on your schedule, but to schedule your priorities."**

- **Avoidance of Overwork**

  While meeting deadlines and fulfilling responsibilities are essential, requiring occasional or event-driven overwork, it's crucial not to let overworking become a habit as it can lead to burnout and have a negative impact on your well-being. Remember to take short breaks, as they can help recharge your energy and improve focus.

- **Leverage Organization Initiatives**

  Often, we don't fully appreciate or utilize the resources and facilities provided by our organizations. Some employees may not even be aware of all the benefits or understand how specific programs operate. Therefore, it's essential to acquaint yourself with what's on offer and utilize these resources according to individual needs as they can greatly aid in achieving a more balanced work-life experience.

- **Prioritize Health**

  Adopt stress-reduction techniques such as meditation, deep breathing exercises, or yoga to manage stress effectively. Regular physical activity is essential for overall well-being, so stay active. Incorporate exercise into your routine, even if it's as simple as a short walk during breaks. Unplugging from electronic devices during personal time can also significantly aid in maintaining balance.

- **Communicate**

  Never assume that your colleagues, managers, or stakeholders understand your priorities, needs, or situations. If you require a flexible work arrangement, approach your manager about it, regardless of whether it's a standard offering at the organizational level. If you're facing challenges, initiate an open and honest conversation with your manager. If you are a manager yourself, having such conversations about clear expectations, goals, and feedback can be extremely helpful. When possible, delegate tasks to reduce your workload. Sharing goals, expectations, and challenges leads to better understanding, increased support, and more effective solutions.

- **Seek Support**

  Don't hesitate to ask for help when you're trying to balance personal commitments with work. Family, friends, or support groups can provide invaluable assistance. If you're anticipating serious physical or mental health challenges, don't delay in seeking professional help.

- **ENJOY your work**

  Finally, at the end of the day, what truly matters is whether you're passionate about your work and if you enjoy (most of) what you do. No amount of work-life balance initiatives can offset the draining effect of a job that you don't love.

  Remember the wise words of **Simon Sinek**: **"Working hard for something we don't care about is called stress; working hard for something we love is called passion."**

It's essential to remember that the concept of balance will vary for each individual and may shift over time. What remains important is maintaining an internal dialogue, remaining adaptable, and consistently striving for a holistic sense of fulfillment.

Reflections on the Practicality of Work-Life Balance

In the global tech context, achieving work-life balance is both complex and vital. Work-life integration is a personal journey, and what works for one person may not work for another—individual needs, circumstances, job roles, and cultural contexts should all be considered. Experiment with different strategies, and find a balance that suits your needs and lifestyle. It's absolutely fine to adjust and adapt your approach as your circumstances change.

Emerging Trends: The Future of Work-Life Balance in the Tech Industry

According to **HR Vision:**

> "Work-life balance is shifting to work-life integration."
>
> "Companies that prioritize work-life integration are more likely to **attract and retain top talent**, as employees recognize the value placed on their personal lives and the flexibility that allows them to excel in their professional roles."

The future of work-life balance in the tech industry is shaped by several emerging trends. The momentum is shifting towards remote and flexible work, which could escalate the adoption of "hybrid" work models. Concurrently, growing awareness about mental health has made employee well-being a top priority for employers.

Technological advancements like AI and automation also promise to redefine work-life integration. These tools could potentially lessen workloads and aid in improving employees' mental health. For example, a virtual AI assistant could help manage employees' mental health concerns proactively by helping them manage stress and anxiety at work every day, thereby bolstering productivity and enhancing overall work-life integration.

Emerging trends also include "workations," a blend of work and vacation, symbolizing the evolving nature of work-life balance. Additionally, new work modalities enabled by virtual reality (VR) and augmented reality (AR) could offer greater flexibility and stress reduction.

The crux lies in how technology is utilized. Companies must intentionally deploy technology to enhance work-life integration rather than hinder it. This mindful application of technology could well define the future of work-life balance in the tech industry.

As we bridge to Chapter 8, it becomes evident that balance isn't solely about melding professional and personal domains; it's intrinsically tied to one's inner world.

The quest for ambition should never be at the expense of one's mental fortitude. Here, we assert the critical importance of self-care, painting it not as an option but as an imperative. Join us as we delve deeper into the self-care mandate, illuminating its role in ensuring unwavering professional excellence.

Chapter Summary

- The concept of work-life balance has evolved from a clear boundary between work and personal life to a more integrated, individualized approach.
- Professional success can be achieved without sacrificing personal fulfillment.
- Employers are becoming active facilitators in the quest for work-life balance for employees and are taking various creative initiatives, including revised policies and culture.
- Employees have to take responsibility and conscious action to enhance their work-life integration by leveraging the facilities provided by their organizations.
- Employer initiatives promoting work-life balance contribute to increased job satisfaction and enhanced productivity and are more likely to attract and retain top talent.
- Future opportunities for work-life balance include increased use of AI/ML to reduce workload, virtual AI assistants to manage day-to-day stress proactively, AR/VR enhancing workplace experience, and trends like workations, a blend of work and vacation.
- Organizational leaders will play a crucial role in shaping the future of work-life balance by setting the tone for the organization's culture, managing changing work landscapes, and modeling healthy work-life balance behaviors.

Chapter 8

The Self-Care Mandate: Prioritizing Mental Well-Being Amidst Ambition

Imagine a bustling corporate office at the end of the quarter. The air is charged with tension as sales teams scramble to meet their quotas, operations teams work diligently to ensure every transaction goes through smoothly, and the systems team logs extra hours due to a high volume of transactions that are slowing systems down. Amidst this whirlwind of activity, there's Sam.

Sam takes a break to eat a nutritious lunch, despite the frenzy. A few hours later, he steps out for a brisk walk to clear his mind. And when the late hours start creeping in, he delegates his system monitoring duties to a night-shift colleague, ensuring he gets a good night's sleep.

The next day, Sam strides into the office well-rested, looking smart and well-groomed, ready to tackle the tasks of the day with full force.

Around him, whispers start to spread. Some label him as selfish, others question his dedication. They wonder how he can stick to his lunch breaks, indulge in short respites, sleep for a full seven hours, and even take the time to look good amidst all the chaos and during such a demanding time—quarter end!

Does Sam's behavior make him a less committed employee? Is he lacking dedication and prioritizing his needs in the midst of high-stakes workdays? It's understandable if your answer is yes.

This common misconception is far from the truth. Self-care, even during highly stressful days at work, is not a selfish act. It is a vital part of maintaining and sustaining good health and a vibrant life.

Driven by Ambition: The Balance of Hustle and Self-Care

Most of the tech workforce, if not all, are very ambitious. Ambition is what makes us push ourselves to achieve our goals and grow in our careers. But it can also push us beyond our limits, which might lead us to health issues, both physical and mental. Self-care is about finding that balance between ambition and well-being, integrating the two, and ensuring that we are able to sustain growth. Thus, taking time out for self-care is not a sign of weakness or lack of dedication or even mean that one is not ambitious. On the contrary, prioritizing self-care is our commitment to ourselves for sustainable success along with well-being.

The Essentials of Self-Care

Similar to work-life integration, which was explained in the previous chapter, self-care is not a one-size-fits-all concept either. It's highly

individual, encompassing a wide range of activities that might enhance long-term physical, mental, and emotional health. It's important to understand that self-care is not a sporadic or one-off activity but a conscious and continuous process of making our choices to lead a balanced, healthy, fulfilling life. It is about taking care of the needs of body and mind and taking steps to meet those needs in a positive, nurturing manner.

The journey towards prioritizing self-care amidst ambition starts now, with understanding and implementing the five basic pillars of self-care—Sleep, Nutrition, Exercise, Mindfulness and often overlooked aspect – Self-presentation.

1. Sleep: The Foundation of Mental Well-Being

Sleep, the first and foremost self-care essential, has the power to make or break the mental fortitude of an individual. Take, for instance, Arianna Huffington, the cofounder and former editor-in-chief of the *Huffington Post*. After collapsing from exhaustion and sleep deprivation, Huffington had an epiphany. She subsequently championed the cause of sleep, penning the bestselling book *The Sleep Revolution* and asserting that sleep deprivation was "the new smoking." In the modern corporate culture, sleep is gradually gaining recognition as a non-negotiable component of success and well-being, though often, it does not get the attention it requires, and sleep deprivation is taken for granted.

The importance of sleep becomes particularly evident when we understand the impacts of sleep deprivation. Chronic lack of sleep can significantly impact cognitive abilities such as focus, attention, concentration, decision-making, and problem-solving. This could, in turn, impact productivity and performance, both in personal as well as professional endeavors.

Furthermore, sleep deprivation can have detrimental effects on our emotional well-being and could lead to mood swings, decreased motivation, increased stress, and heightened vulnerability to psychological conditions.

Thus, quality sleep is a crucial pillar of self-care. It helps regulate mood, fosters resilience to stress, and contributes to a positive outlook on life. By acknowledging its importance and actively working to improve our sleep hygiene, we can lay a strong foundation for improved mental well-being and performance. The ripple effects of good sleep reach far into every aspect of our lives, reinforcing the truth in the adage, "Sleep is the best meditation."

Recently, Bill Gates, who once believed "sleep is laziness and unnecessary," revealed that he now paid close attention to his daily sleep score, recognizing that quality rest was essential. He also said, "One of the most predictive factors of any dementia, including Alzheimer's, is whether you're getting good sleep."

2. Nutrition: Fuel for the Mind and Body

The axiom, "You are what you eat," has a new meaning. A landmark study published in the *American Journal of Psychiatry* revealed a significant correlation between dietary patterns and mental health. There is extensive research showing that individuals who eat processed food, refined sugars, or unhealthy fats are prone to depression and anxiety while those who eat foods like fruits, vegetables, and lean proteins have lower mental health risks. Acknowledging this, many corporate giants sport on-campus cafeterias that offer balanced, wholesome meals, reinforcing the significance of nutrition in cognitive function and mental well-being. Maintaining a nutritious diet amidst a busy lifestyle may seem challenging, but with a bit of planning and conscious effort, it is entirely feasible. This might mean planning and preparing wholesome food for daily meals, being conscious about portion control, and more importantly, deliberately choosing healthy snacks, which might be extremely difficult, especially if you are sitting on long calls or working late hours after dinner when you really start to feel hungry again well before going to bed!

3. Exercise: Boosting Physical and Mental Fitness

In a study led by **Dr. Andrea Dunn** at the **Cooper Institute in Dallas, regular exercise was found to reduce symptoms of depression by 47%**.

Physical activity triggers the release of endorphins—our body's natural mood elevators—leading to the "feel-good" sensation often experienced after a workout. It also enhances the brain's sensitivity to the hormones serotonin and norepinephrine, which relieve feelings of depression and anxiety.

Additionally, exercise promotes better sleep, which, in turn, can improve mood and decrease stress levels. It also provides a natural and healthy way to cope with stress as physical activity reduces the levels of stress hormones in the body.

So, make it a priority and find time for workouts, even if it is 20 minutes of brisk walking to start with, or it can be in any other form you enjoy—yoga, Zumba, dancing, running, swimming, or aerobics. Short bursts of high-intensity interval training (HIIT) workouts would do as well!

4. Mindfulness: Finding Calm Amidst the Chaos

In the relentless hustle of modern life, we often find ourselves multitasking and juggling multiple responsibilities all the time. This perpetual state of "doing something" or the other all the time might make us lose focus on the "present moment," leading to mental well-being challenges.

This is where mindfulness is extremely useful—by intentionally focusing on the present moment in a non-judgmental manner. It's about acknowledging and accepting our current moment thoughts, feelings, and sensations as they arise, thus helping us to respond to stressful situations rather than reacting and building emotional resilience.

Consider **Bill George, the former CEO of Medtronic,** who credits mindfulness meditation as a catalyst in his transformation into an authentic leader. Today, he teaches mindfulness practices to business students at Harvard, shaping the leaders of tomorrow.

The benefits of mindfulness are manifold, particularly in relation to mental health. A study conducted by researchers at **Johns Hopkins** found evidence of a link between mindfulness and reduced anxiety, depression, and pain. Additionally, **a meta-analysis of studies by the University of Surrey** suggested that **mindfulness in the workplace could decrease stress and improve resilience, emotional intelligence, and job satisfaction**.

Practicing mindfulness doesn't require too much time, commitment, or daily lifestyle changes. It can be as simple as 10–15 minutes of mindful breathing or body scan technique or guided meditation. Considering the benefits, I am sure we can spare 10–15 minutes for practicing mindfulness every day!

Regular mindfulness practice can bring a host of long-term benefits. Studies have shown that it can reduce stress, improve attention and memory, enhance emotional regulation, boost self-esteem, and even foster empathy and compassion.

Moreover, by cultivating a more mindful approach to life, we can derive more joy and satisfaction from our daily activities and improve our relationships. We can learn to appreciate the simple moments of life and respond to life's challenges with greater calm and clarity.

5. Self-Presentation: Dressing and Grooming for Success

An often overlooked aspect, especially with remote working, is the power of self-presentation. Looking good can significantly impact how we feel about ourselves. Studies have shown that the clothes we wear, our grooming habits, and our overall physical presentation can influence our mood, confidence, and even our performance. It can also serve as an external symbol of our inner well-being.

Self-presentation isn't about conforming to societal beauty standards or impressing others. It's about feeling comfortable, expressing individuality, and presenting ourselves in the best version depending on our preferences, lifestyle, and self-expression. This will enhance self-image, and more importantly, self-efficacy. Dressing and grooming set the tone for the day and also send a positive message that we value and respect ourselves.

Self-presentation, even in the context of remote working, holds a significant value. Engaging in these routines can boost self-confidence, set clear boundaries between work and leisure, and maintain professionalism during video calls. These practices not only establish a productive mindset but also promote positive self-perception, ensuring readiness for unplanned interactions. In essence, even in the flexibility of work-from-home setups, personal presentation remains a potent tool for enhancing focus, asserting individuality, and fostering a sense of normalcy. So, don't feel guilty about setting aside a small portion of your earnings for self-presentation!

First Aid for the Mind: Seeking Help at the Right Time

I firmly believe that mental health requires proactive attention just like physical health. Just like how we have first aid for minor physical injuries before rushing to a hospital, we need a "first aid" approach to mental health. In the workplace, where we have daily challenges causing tension, stress, and anxiety, having immediate access to tools or resources, like, let's say a "mental health first aid provider," can be invaluable. Imagine a future workplace where a virtual AI buddy is available 24x7, interacts with employees, and understands their daily work routines, as well as how they are doing on self-care pillars, acts as employees' first line of defense, offering immediate support and coping strategies for the challenges they run into throughout the day. This would greatly help employees not to prolong their issues, and arrest the challenge before it gets bigger.

Though most of the minor day-to-day work challenges causing stress can be addressed through preliminary assistance, it's crucial to recognize the limits and boundaries of such "first aid" assistance. Just like persistent physical pain requires a doctor's visit, if your mental distress exacerbates or is prolonged, you should immediately seek professional help from psychologists, counselors, or therapists. There should not be any stigma or hesitation to seek professional help just like how you wouldn't hesitate to immediately seek a doctor for physical ailments.

This dual approach, combining immediate preliminary support with the option to seek professional intervention as and when necessary, enables a comprehensive approach to sustaining mental health.

When and Why to Seek Professional Help

Identifying when to seek professional help can be challenging. If you're experiencing persistent sadness, anxiety, irritability, or significant distress that interferes with work or your personal life, it may be time to seek professional help. Other signs could include feeling disconnected or distant from others, experiencing unexplained physical ailments, having thoughts of self-harm or suicide, or it can even be that the preliminary assistance provided by AI buddy (if you are using one or your organization provides one in the future) is not working.

Seeking professional help can provide the support needed to navigate difficult life experiences and manage serious mental health conditions. Mental health professionals can provide a fresh perspective on a difficult problem, guide you towards potential solutions, or provide coping strategies; a psychiatrist can even put you on medications. Just remember that it's okay to reach out for help when needed; there should not be hesitation or stigma whatsoever.

Company Policies and Initiatives: Support for Mental Health

We have already discussed in detail different policies, cultures, or initiatives that organizations are taking up when it comes to work-life integration. Mental health-related initiatives are part of work-life integration. Employers are increasingly playing a critical role in promoting employees' mental well-being as there is a strong realization that positive mental health can enhance productivity, creativity, and overall job satisfaction, contributing to a more engaged and motivated workforce and eventually contributing to the company's success.

Below are some effective company policies and practices specific to mental health.

- **Mental Health Awareness and Training**

  Organizations are providing resources, workshops, and sessions to spread awareness about mental health to their employees. They are also providing training to managers/leaders to identify and help manage the mental health struggles of their teams and respond compassionately.

- **Employee Assistance Programs**

  Organizations have embraced various EAP platforms where confidential counseling services are being provided by psychologists, some even 24x7, helping employees deal with serious personal or work-related mental health issues. These programs are often offered to employees' family members as well.

- **Mental Health Days**

  Some companies have started to offer mental health days as part of their sick leave policy, acknowledging that mental health is just as important as physical health.

- **Mindfulness and Wellness Programs**

  These might include offering mindfulness training, fitness programs, or access to wellness apps.

  In the near future, when AI buddies—first aid mental health providers—become available, I am sure companies won't hesitate to explore and embrace them if it is going to add value to employees.

Advocating for Mental Health Initiatives in Your Workplace

If your workplace doesn't yet have mental health support policies in place, consider becoming an advocate. This could involve raising awareness about the importance of mental health, encouraging open dialogue about mental health issues, proposing specific initiatives such as those listed above, or being on top of the latest tech advancements/start-ups on mental health management and exploring those.

Personalized Self-Care Plan: Time for Action

Creating a personalized self-care plan is a powerful way to take ownership of your mental health. The beauty of such a plan is that it's tailored to your unique needs, lifestyle, and goals, making it more likely to be effective and sustainable instead of a generic one.

The first step is to assess your mental health needs, which requires honest self-reflection and awareness. Key areas to consider are how you are doing on the five pillars of mental health described above, your stress levels, your work-life integration preferences, and your coping mechanisms. Even if your work-life preferences are overambitious on the work side, just remember that it shouldn't come at the cost of your mental health. Setting realistic and achievable goals can help ensure that your ambition fuels you rather than depleting you.

Once you have done the self-assessment and have your goals set, it's time to put those into action.

Remember, self-care isn't a one-size-fits-all approach, and it's okay to make adjustments as needed. Regularly review your plan and make modifications based on your evolving needs and circumstances. Don't be discouraged by setbacks. Instead, view them as opportunities for learning and adaptation. Celebrate your successes, no matter how small they may seem. Every step forward is progress toward better mental health.

Self-Care for Women: A Special Note

Women often face unique challenges when focusing on self-care. This could be due to societal and cultural expectations or even just the natural caring instinct for others that makes them focus on the needs of the family before their own. This tendency often impacts their mental and physical health negatively.

Many women often multitask, juggle various personal responsibilities, and have a disproportionate amount of household chores, especially mothers. This can leave no time for self-care, potentially leading to stress and burnout.

It is critical for women to consciously focus and incorporate self-care into their routines no matter what phase of life they are in. This may involve setting boundaries, delegating tasks, simply allowing themselves to take time out for relaxation and rejuvenation, seeking help from others, and more importantly, accepting help, when offered, without feeling guilty.

I have also often noticed that women don't let go! It's okay to let go and not expect everything to be perfect. Women should remember that it's not selfish to spend a portion of their money on self-presentation—dressing, grooming, skin care, etc. In fact, it's only when we take care of ourselves that we can effectively care for others.

Women will have some unique needs during hormonal changes, pregnancy, postpartum recovery, returning to work from maternity leave, and menopause, which should all be considered during the self-care plan and action.

Self-Care for Consultants on the Move: A Balancing Act

Consultants who frequently move from one customer location to another face unique challenges when it comes to self-care. Their constantly changing environments, demanding schedules, and the need to adapt to various customer cultures or just adapting to different dress codes can take a toll on their mental and physical well-being. The very nature of their job may perpetuate a culture where self-care takes a backseat, leaving them susceptible to burnout and overall diminished well-being.

Below are some specific self-care tips.

- **Prioritize Sleep**

  Traveling and adjusting to different time zones can disrupt sleep patterns. It's crucial for consultants to prioritize sleep and create a consistent bedtime routine, ensuring they get enough rest even if their schedules are tight, like having to take customers out for dinner, etc.

- **Make Time for Family and Relationships**

  Frequent travel and long work hours may lead to limited family time, especially on weekdays. It's essential for consultants to make an effort to stay connected with loved ones. Scheduling regular calls or video chats can help maintain strong relationships despite the distance. Give a lot more importance to family time over the weekends.

- **Utilize Downtime Wisely**

  While on the road, consultants may have moments of downtime between meetings and appointments. Instead of using this time for work-related tasks, they should dedicate it to self-care activities, practicing mindfulness such as meditation, reading, or engaging in a hobby they enjoy.

- **Embrace Flexible Dressing**

  With varying client dress codes, consultants may find themselves switching between formal attire one week and casual wear the next. They should embrace the flexibility and use it as an opportunity to express personal style while still respecting the client's culture and expectations.

- **Pack Nutritious Snacks**

  Constant travel can lead to unhealthy eating habits. Packing nutritious snacks and consciously opting for healthier meal options when available can help maintain energy levels and overall well-being.

- **Stay Hydrated**

  Drinking enough water is crucial, especially during travel. Consultants should make a conscious effort to stay hydrated despite their busy schedules.

- **Incorporate Exercise**

  Finding time to exercise on the road may be challenging, but it's essential for physical and mental health. Even short workouts, like stretching or brisk walking, can make a significant difference.

- **Allow for Rest and Recovery**

  After intense projects or extended travel, consultants should give themselves time to rest and recover. Taking breaks between assignments is essential for recharging and avoiding burnout.

In conclusion, consultants who frequently move from one customer location to another lead demanding lives that require intentional self-care. By prioritizing sleep, setting boundaries, embracing flexibility, and making time for personal well-being, they can maintain balance and thrive in their careers while safeguarding their health and happiness.

Self-Care for Senior Leaders: Leading from the Front

In an organization, every employee is a leader in one capacity or another. However, senior leaders within organizations often bear an augmented weight of responsibilities, making their journey laden with unique stressors. Much like aircraft protocol, which emphasizes securing one's oxygen mask before assisting others, senior leaders must prioritize their well-being to be able to effectively guide their teams. This principle isn't rooted in selfishness but in survival; it's a recognition that optimal self-care directly translates to optimal leadership. The higher the role in the organization ladder, the lonelier the path may become. Often, senior leaders are privy to information they cannot always share—the potential pitfalls in a company's future, looming performance declines, or even potential job losses. These burdens are often shouldered in silence, intensifying the mental strain. Given the magnitude of their responsibilities, it becomes paramount for senior leaders to consciously invest in their mental health, ensuring they remain resilient pillars of strength for their teams and organizations.

In summary, as we continue to strive and thrive, let's ensure that self-care remains a priority. Let's remember that we deserve to take care of ourselves, not only for our mental well-being but also for the fulfillment of our ambitions. As we move forward, let's commit to prioritizing our mental health, fostering a sustainable balance between ambition and self-care, and creating a culture that values and respects mental well-being.

We underscored self-care as more than a mere act of rejuvenation; it stands as a pillar of both professional tenacity and personal well-being. Yet, as we transition to Chapter 9, our focus narrows to a group often celebrated for their visionary drive yet seldom acknowledged for their silent mental struggles: **entrepreneurs**.

Chapter Summary

- Embracing self-care is non-negotiable in today's high-pressure environments, impacting not just personal but also professional efficacy.
- Comprehensive self-care integrates sleep, nutrition, exercise, mindfulness, and self-presence to fortify mental well-being.
- Proactively address mental health challenges as "first aid" before they escalate, ensuring consistent mental strength and resilience.
- Envision advanced tools like AI buddies as round-the-clock mental health allies, offering self-care plans, immediate coping strategies, and support.
- At elevated organizational levels, self-care becomes paramount, ensuring leaders remain resilient pillars amidst heightened responsibilities.
- In the age of virtual work, grooming and dressing still hold significance, driving productivity, self-worth, and maintaining professional standards.
- Recognize and respect the boundary between self-help and the crucial need for expert care, ensuring timely and appropriate professional mental health interventions.
- Champion workplace policies that prioritize employee mental health, cultivating a supportive, balanced environment.
- Every individual's self-care journey is unique; crafting and adapting a personal plan ensures a balance between ambition and well-being.
- Self-care isn't merely a personal indulgence; it's the foundation of sustained success, professional growth, and a balanced life.

Chapter 9

The Entrepreneurial Journey: Balancing Innovation, Passion, and Mental Health

Why are we having a separate chapter on entrepreneurs? Because entrepreneurs are increasing, and they are unique; so are their challenges.

> *There were* ***five million*** new businesses created in 2022.
>
> —*Gusto*

Let's think of words that come to our mind when we think of entrepreneurs.

Some of the words that leap into my mind are bold, adventurous, intelligent, risk-takers, passionate, and innovative mindset. From the outside, the entrepreneurial journey often appears to be a glamorous adventure, a crusade paved with innovative ideas, ceaseless passion, trailblazing achievements, fame, and success. But being the spouse of a serial entrepreneur and having many entrepreneurs in my circle, I know that beneath this exhilarating façade lies an untold story—a tale of uncertainties, unseen pressures, unspoken fears, and unheard struggles.

Just as an iceberg hides its most significant part beneath the water's surface, entrepreneurship, too, veils a substantial portion of its reality below the triumphant headlines and success stories. The relentless work without any boundaries of day/night or weekdays/weekends or holidays, constant uncertainties, the poignant solitude, and the profound mental toll—these form the invisible narrative of entrepreneurship, often concealed behind the start-up success saga.

From the immense pressure to succeed and the lonely path of innovation to the constant juggling between work and personal life, let's delve into the realities of the entrepreneurial lifestyle and how it impacts their mental health. It is not about just the hardships but about how to pave the path to balance, resilience, and well-being, guiding entrepreneurs on harmonizing innovation, passion, and mental health. Because the entrepreneurial journey isn't just about creating successful businesses but also about fostering successful, balanced entrepreneurs.

A study conducted by the **University of California, San Francisco** revealed that **entrepreneurs are 50% more likely to report having a mental health condition**.

The Entrepreneurial Lifestyle: Passion and Pressure

Entrepreneurs are driven to bring innovative ideas to life, solve unique customer or industry problems creatively, disrupt the status quo, and create lasting impact. So, entrepreneurship demands unwavering commitment, ceaseless dedication, and boundless passion. This pursuit often becomes their identity, blurring the lines between their personal and professional selves.

However, the same passion that fuels entrepreneurial fire can also be the catalyst for immense pressure. Irrespective of which phase they are in, entrepreneurs find themselves in a relentless race against time, competitors, and market dynamics. From conceptualizing an idea to delivering a minimum viable product, from doing customer validations to finding investors, from assembling a team to building the full product or service, from market research to full-blown lead generation to sales, they are constantly juggling a myriad of responsibilities.

The enormous weight of these expectations, often self-imposed, can lead to long working hours, erratic schedules, constant multitasking, and a relentless work pace, leaving little to no time for personal life and self-care. The constant hustle and bustle of this lifestyle can feel isolating, exacerbating feelings of stress, anxiety, and even leading to very quick burnout, physically, emotionally, as well as financially.

The pressure to succeed and the fear of failure can take a toll, with every setback or challenge magnified in the entrepreneurial echo chamber. It becomes crucial to acknowledge that while passion is a driving force, it can also contribute to the mental health challenges many entrepreneurs face.

Understanding this delicate balance between passion and pressure and being prepared are key to managing mental well-being in the entrepreneurial world. Navigating this landscape involves recognizing the signs of mental distress, setting clear boundaries, and promoting a culture of well-being, which we will explore further in the sections to follow.

Unique Challenges: Struggles, Responsibilities, and Obligations

Entrepreneurship, while rewarding, comes with a unique set of stressors that can place entrepreneurs at a higher risk for certain mental health issues. The blend of **personal commitment, financial**

risk, uncertain outcomes, and high-stakes decision-making creates an environment ripe for psychological strain.

One of the primary concerns is the isolation that entrepreneurs often face. Launching and running a start-up can be a lonely journey, especially when starting out. The loneliness is more intense if there are no cofounders. The weight of making critical decisions alone, coupled with the immense responsibility of steering the venture towards success, can create a sense of loneliness that contributes to stress and anxiety.

The concerns vary when entrepreneurs navigate their journey with cofounders, bringing into play the dynamics of collaboration, conflict resolution, decision-making, and shared responsibility. The pressure escalates when these challenges need to be tackled in an environment of financial uncertainty or instability.

An added layer of stress might emanate from the funding sources of the start-up. When initial funds are raised from family and friends, entrepreneurs often grapple with a sense of immense responsibility and obligation. This funding structure converts personal relationships into professional ones, blurring boundaries and amplifying the potential for conflict and stress. The fear of letting down close ones, and the worry of jeopardizing personal relationships, can add to the entrepreneur's mental strain.

Financial instability is another significant factor. The uncertainty of income, the pressure to secure funding, increased expenses,—including payroll, infrastructure cost, customer acquisition cost, etc.—and the responsibility of financial decisions impacting not just the entrepreneur but also their team can lead to sleep disorders, anxiety, and even depression.

The high-stakes environment of entrepreneurship can amplify the impact of failures and setbacks. Every decision an entrepreneur makes can potentially make or break their business, leading to a constant state of high alert and stress. This chronic stress can manifest itself in various forms, including burnout, anxiety disorders, and depression.

Moreover, while working relentlessly towards ambitious goals in high-stakes environments, entrepreneurs frequently find themselves facing intense pressures. These might stem from various sources—sustaining business growth, managing investor expectations, tackling competition, keeping up with market trends, maintaining customer satisfaction, or securing further investments. Combined, these factors contribute to a high-stress environment that can lead to burnout, anxiety, and other mental health issues if not properly managed

The blurred lines between personal and professional life can also contribute to an imbalance, leading to the neglect of personal health, relationships, and leisure activities. This imbalance can exacerbate feelings of being overwhelmed, increasing the risk of burnout and other mental health issues.

Finally, the stigma associated with mental health, coupled with the expectation of the relentlessly passionate and tireless entrepreneur, can prevent individuals from seeking help. This silence can worsen mental health conditions, leading to a cycle of distress.

Recognizing these unique challenges is the first step towards understanding the intricacies of mental health in the entrepreneurial context. With this understanding, we can then explore strategies and solutions tailored to this unique group.

Let's delve deeper into the myriad uncertainties that entrepreneurs must tackle and how these can be managed and mitigated to foster a healthy mental state.

Entrepreneurship's Fog: The Shadows of Uncertainty

Uncertainty is an inseparable companion on the entrepreneurial journey. It lurks in every corner, from establishing product-market fit to securing financial sustainability to building the product through the entire customer life cycle, casting long shadows of stress and anxiety. Let's explore how these uncertainties act as formidable mental health challenges for entrepreneurs.

Proof of concept (PoC) and minimum viable product (MVP) development are pivotal steps in the entrepreneurial process. Uncertainty about the expenditure on PoC, clear MVP outcomes, and decisions about whether to continue with a specific start-up (or not) can be major sources of anxiety for entrepreneurs. Allocating the right amount of spend on these stages without a concrete guarantee of success can be an immense source of stress. Any miscalculations could lead not just to financial losses but could also potentially jeopardize the entire venture.

Fear of missing market relevance is another lurking uncertainty. The rapid pace of technological advancements and evolving customer preferences means that entrepreneurs are in a constant race against time. The stress of staying ahead and differentiating against competition, innovating continually, and preventing their product or service from becoming obsolete can be a significant mental toll.

The overarching fear of running out of funds amplifies these uncertainties. Financial instability is a reality for many entrepreneurs, especially in the early stages. The pressure to remain solvent, pay employees, and move towards a positive return on investment (ROI) while keeping the business afloat can lead to chronic stress and anxiety, affecting overall mental well-being.

When entrepreneurs accept funding from venture capitalists or other investors, they take on a new level of responsibility. These investors are looking for a return on their investment as quickly as possible and may have specific expectations regarding the company's pace of growth and performance. This can place additional pressure on entrepreneurs and heighten anxiety levels.

Managing these pressures involves open communication, setting realistic expectations with investors, and maintaining a disciplined approach towards financial management. This includes accepting invalidated MVP results, having the courage to pivot when necessary, and avoiding false beliefs about guaranteed success.

About **90%** of start-ups fail.

—Failory

In essence, the entrepreneurial journey is a roller coaster ride through the shadows of uncertainty. It's crucial to shed light on these aspects, acknowledging their impact on mental health and exploring strategies to navigate this challenging landscape.

Resilience: A Key Trait and the Lure of Serial Entrepreneurship

For entrepreneurs, resilience is much more than just a buzzword; it's an essential trait for survival. As the captains of their ships, entrepreneurs often sail against strong winds of setbacks and failures. However, resilience is the anchor that keeps them steady in these stormy seas.

Resilience, an entrepreneur's secret weapon, is more than just recovery; it is the strength to march forward, grow through challenges, fall and rise again, face failure, learn from mistakes but keep moving, and come back strong with another spark of an idea. This tenacity explains why the world witnesses a fascinating phenomenon—serial entrepreneurship. Despite experiencing the arduous journey of entrepreneurship, entrepreneurs find themselves back on the starting line, ready to launch into a new venture if their idea fails OR they bring their current venture to any logical point of exit, etc. It's this allure of the thrill, the joy of creation, the hope of making an impact, and the spirit of innovation that keeps them drawn to the entrepreneurial world, even when a seemingly comfortable corporate life awaits.

Often, this resilience arises from deep-seated passion, belief in their ideas, and confidence in making an impact, tempered by the previous stumbles and enriched by the lessons learned. The unflinching will to make a difference, the pursuit of solutions, and the desire to create value for customers often outweigh the lure of a safer, more predictable path. Every new venture, with all its challenges, represents a fresh canvas for their ideas, further strengthening their mental fortitude.

Moreover, the experience of leading a venture, the autonomy it offers, the potential impact it promises, and the potential non-linear growth opportunities it creates often make returning to the corporate world less appealing for many entrepreneurs. While the entrepreneurial path is strewn with obstacles, it also offers an unmatched opportunity to shape one's destiny and bring a vision to life. This opportunity, combined with the resilience honed through their journey, fuels entrepreneurs to start again, venturing into the cycle of challenges with an empowered mindset and fortified resolve.

It is essential, however, to note that resilience isn't an inborn trait but a cultivated skill. It can be fostered by focusing on mental well-being, learning from past experiences, and drawing on resources and support systems available. Let's explore how entrepreneurs can build and enhance this crucial trait.

Strategies for Building Resilience

Building resilience is an ongoing process, not a one-time effort. Here are some practical strategies to cultivate this invaluable trait.

- **Early realization:** Understand that failure is a part of the process. Not every MVP will yield the desired results. Maintain the discipline to accept invalidated results and be prepared to pivot, if necessary, early on in the venture process. This might cause anxiety initially but will spare you from bigger emotional stress (and many other unwanted factors) in the long run.

- **Investor updates:** It's important to regularly update all investors about the start-up's progress. This demonstrates transparency and respect for their investment and can mitigate feelings of burden. If the start-up encounters setbacks, these should be communicated honestly. This open communication can help manage expectations and ensure that all investors are on the same page, reducing the potential for misunderstanding and conflict. More importantly, it saves the entrepreneur from a lot of stress and anxiety.

- **Remove guilt:** While entrepreneurs have a responsibility towards their investors, it is also essential not to be overly burdened by feelings of guilt or obligation if the initial investment has come from family and friends. It's natural to feel some level of personal pressure and obligation, but it's also important to remember that all investments carry risk, and those who invest in start-ups are typically aware of this. If they are not, please ensure clear expectations are set from the very outset. Providing upfront expectations about potential risks helps in fostering understanding and patience and retaining personal bonds.
- **Foster a growth mindset:** Cultivate an attitude that embraces challenges as opportunities for learning and growth. This mindset shift can transform setbacks into stepping stones, fueling your journey forward.
- **Be agile:** It's important to stay nimble and adapt to changes. Pivot your use cases, market positioning, solutioning, etc., if necessary, based on technology trends, the market situation, customer feedback, the competitive landscape, and changing needs in the industry itself.
- **Leverage your support system:** Don't isolate yourself. Start-up communities like NASSCOM or San Francisco entrepreneurship clubs help entrepreneurs become successful. Reach out to mentors, peers, friends, or family members who can provide emotional support, valuable advice, or a different perspective. Remember, a problem shared is a problem halved.
- **Maintain physical health:** Regular exercise, a balanced diet, and adequate sleep form the three pillars of physical well-being. Neglecting physical health can intensify stress and impede mental resilience.

- **Manage financial stress:** Be proactive in financial planning. Maintain a strict budget and have a contingency plan. Mitigating financial stress can free your mind to focus on innovation and problem-solving, strengthening your resilience.

  In 2023, 82% of businesses that went under did so because of cash flow problems.

  —Fundera

- **Avoid false beliefs:** Don't fall into the trap of the sunk cost fallacy—the mistaken belief that you should continue with an endeavor because of the time, money, and resources already invested, despite witnessing that they are not yielding results. Recognize when to let go, pivot, or change course.
- **Customer demands:** As the start-up moves to the growth stage and more customers start to use the product, pressure from customers to take up new product features will increase. Balance customer expansion with the strategic product vision. Take up the additional features only if it aligns with the strategic product vision and/or the features can be broadly adopted across the customer base.
- **Learn to delegate:** One of the biggest traps for entrepreneurs is the belief that they must do everything themselves. Learn to delegate tasks that can be managed by others. This can free up your time, reduce stress, and enable you to focus on strategic aspects of your venture.
- **Expect the unexpected:** Entrepreneurs often experience the unpredictable waters of funding and customer invoices. While investors may verbally commit to funding, the actual disbursement can be significantly delayed. Similarly, customer payments may not arrive as promptly as anticipated. To safeguard against these uncertainties, wise entrepreneurs plan ahead with a buffer of at least three months, assuming potential delays in funding or payments, and also have a high-level plan B for alternate funding arrangements if there

are any last-minute surprises. This preparation reduces the tremendous pressure that arises when faced with last-minute funding setbacks or sudden changes.

Building resilience is akin to constructing a sturdy ship capable of withstanding the tumultuous entrepreneurial voyage. It's about understanding that even amidst the storm, you're learning, growing, and becoming better equipped for the journey ahead.

Setting Boundaries: The Work-Life Balance Act and the Role of Family

Entrepreneurs often find that the lines between work and personal life blur as they pour their energy and time into building their businesses. This intense commitment can lead to sacrifices not just by entrepreneurs themselves but also by their immediate family members, who provide invaluable support.

Family members often play unsung roles in an entrepreneur's journey, whether it's providing emotional support, taking on increased household responsibilities, helping with finances, or even sacrificing comforts. Acknowledging this contribution and understanding the potential strains entrepreneurship can place on family life is crucial.

For entrepreneurs, it's vital to set clear boundaries to ensure their work does not consume their entire lives and overshadow their relationships. Strategies to maintain this balance can include setting specific work hours, creating separate workspaces at home, and consciously setting aside quality time for the family.

It's also important for entrepreneurs to keep their families informed about their work and its challenges, not only to manage expectations but also to help family members feel included and appreciated.

By setting firm boundaries, entrepreneurs can maintain their mental well-being while passionately pursuing their entrepreneurial dreams. After all, the entrepreneur's journey isn't a sprint; it's a marathon.

Seeking Help: Breaking the Stigma and Embracing Resources

It's not uncommon for entrepreneurs to wear their stress like a badge of honor. The high-pressure world of start-ups often romanticizes the notion of the tireless, resilient entrepreneur, which can contribute to a stigma around acknowledging mental health challenges. This can breed a culture of silence, causing many entrepreneurs to internalize their struggles rather than seek help.

Many believe that employee assistance programs or AI-powered mental health virtual assistants are the exclusive domain of large corporations. This is a myth. In fact, start-ups and small businesses might benefit from these mental health resources even more than established companies due to the unique stresses and challenges they face.

EAPs and AI tools can provide valuable mental health support for entrepreneurs and their teams, offering services like suggestions on day-to-day work challenges, counseling, stress management programs, and wellness resources. They can help foster a culture of mental well-being even in the high-pressure environment of a start-up.

In a start-up, every team member's contribution is critical, and their mental health is a significant factor in their performance and overall business success. Encouraging a culture that breaks the stigma around mental health and promotes the use of available resources is a mark of enlightened and empathetic entrepreneurial leadership. Embracing an open culture as a start-up has a huge impact on the overall well-being of employees when the start-up grows into a large corporation. So seed the plant of an open culture early on.

As an entrepreneur, you are a changemaker, innovator, and leader, and taking care of your mental health only enhances these qualities. Mental health is not an individual concern; it's a business one, a societal one, and a human one. So, let's prioritize mental health not just for business success but for the holistic success of the entrepreneur.

Chapter Summary

- Entrepreneurship's allure lies in autonomy, potential impact, and the thrill of creation, often surpassing the comfort of corporate life, but it comes with its unique challenges.
- Understanding the delicate balance between passion and pressure and being prepared are key to managing mental well-being in the entrepreneurial world.
- Entrepreneurship, while rewarding, comes with a distinctive set of stressors that can place entrepreneurs at a higher risk for certain mental health issues.
- By setting firm boundaries, entrepreneurs can maintain their mental well-being while passionately pursuing their entrepreneurial dreams.
- Building resilience involves recognizing failure as a learning opportunity, maintaining open investor communication, and proactive financial planning.
- To thrive in the entrepreneurial landscape, one must balance customer demands, delegate effectively, and prepare for financial uncertainties.
- In a start-up, every team member is highly dependent on each other, each one's contribution is critical, and their mental health is a significant factor in their performance and overall business success.
- As an entrepreneur, you are a changemaker, innovator, and leader, and taking care of your mental health only enhances these qualities.
- Prioritize mental health not just for business success but for holistic success as an entrepreneur.

Chapter 10

Looking Ahead: The Resilient Future of the Global Work Landscape

Step into the future, where mental wellness takes center stage in the ever-evolving world of the workplace. As we embrace a new era of employee well-being, mental health support will transform, empowering employees to achieve their best. Let's explore the bold possibilities, from cutting-edge technology to innovative policies, that could help in shaping brighter, more resilient workplaces worldwide in the future.

Minds at Work: Fusing Mental Wellness with Corporate Culture

The first step towards integrating mental wellness into work culture is acknowledging its significance and understanding that mental health challenges are prevalent among employees. While mental wellness is emerging as one of the critical aspects in workplaces, we have a long way to go in completely breaking the stigma surrounding mental health. By breaking the stigma, organizations can foster open conversations about the subject, encouraging employees to seek help without fear of judgment. Employees need to be keen to embrace the culture even more so that organizations can actively listen and understand the potential toll of mental health challenges on individuals and teams and grasp the urgency of addressing the issues.

Future Minds: Leveraging Platforms for Mindful Workspaces

In the ever-developing landscape of work, the integration of modern workplace experiences becomes vital to address the mental health needs of employees effectively. By embracing technological advancements, organizations can offer innovative solutions that cater to various aspects of mental well-being. Recognizing the diverse needs and preferences of the workforce, these platforms could provide personalized support, ensuring every individual feels valued and empowered. Moreover, as remote and virtual work becomes more prevalent, these platforms aid employees in navigating the challenges of the virtual work environment while maintaining their mental wellness.

Proactivity should be the cornerstone of modern workplaces. The platforms will enable organizations to identify potential mental health challenges beforehand and provide preventive measures and resources to address them. As employees experience a supportive work environment that prioritizes their mental well-being, they are more likely to be motivated, resilient, and invested in their roles.

Modern mental wellness platforms equipped with real-time advice capabilities offer employees immediate solutions to cope with daily work challenges. By empowering individuals with timely guidance, employees can better manage stress, anxiety, and workload pressures effectively. Moreover, these platforms aid in enhancing employees' decision-making abilities as they can access relevant resources and support precisely when needed. The agility and adaptability fostered through real-time advice empower the workforce to navigate uncertainties and changes with confidence, contributing to a more resilient and forward-looking organization.

Harnessing AI for Mental Health Boosts

As we continue to embrace technological advancements, leveraging AI assistants for mental health support becomes a promising avenue in the future of work. Virtual AI assistants could play a huge role in providing efficient and personalized mental health support and facilitating employee well-being.

Virtual AI assistants hold tremendous potential to transform mental health support for employees. These AI-powered platforms offer personalized and confidential assistance, ensuring that employees can access support at their convenience and comfort. By intelligently addressing initial assessments and helping manage minor issues, AI assistants can free up human resources, allowing mental health professionals to focus on more complex cases and individualized care. Moreover, these virtual assistants can provide continuous assistance and help employees manage the changes advised by mental health professionals

Technology, when leveraged effectively, can offer valuable data-driven insights for proactive interventions in workplace mental health. AI-powered platforms collect and analyze data to identify patterns and trends, allowing organizations to intervene before issues escalate. By closely monitoring workplace trends, organizations can detect potential challenges and develop strategies to mitigate them. This proactive approach strengthens organizational preparedness and response, fostering resilience in the face of adversities.

AI plays a vital role in facilitating employees' personalized and tailored self-care plans. Employees can access tools, exercises, and resources that align with their specific mental health goals. AI-driven platforms can also track employees' progress, providing valuable feedback and motivation throughout their mental wellness journey. Additionally, AI fosters a culture of continuous learning and improvement by suggesting relevant articles, courses, and activities that promote mental health and overall well-being.

By embracing the potential of virtual AI assistants, organizations can elevate their mental health support, leverage technology to enhance resilience, and facilitate employees' journeys towards holistic well-being. As technology continues to evolve, AI-powered solutions will undoubtedly become pivotal in promoting a mentally healthy and forward-looking workforce.

Evolving Care: Next-Level Wellness Beyond EAPs

While traditional wellness platforms and EAPs have been extremely valuable in raising awareness about mental health and supporting employees with consultations with mental health professionals, some even 24x7, they often fall short in providing personalized proactive care, post-therapy follow-up, progress tracking, and continuous management. Many of these programs have a reactive approach, only offering assistance after employees have experienced mental health challenges.

Looking ahead, organizations must recognize the limitations of standard wellness platforms. They need to move beyond the one-size-fits-all approach and invest in a solution that provides proactive support and daily management and takes into account the unique needs of each employee.

I have come across a couple of start-ups that are close to handling the future needs of employees to manage their mental health and have tremendous potential to truly make an impact.

- **Woebot:** This start-up platform is an automated therapist that aims to use Natural Language programming (NLP) and learned responses to mimic a conversation, remember the past session, and provide advice about sleep, worry, and stress.

- **Wysa:** This is an anxiety therapy chatbot that aims to help people self-manage stress through AI-guided listening and professional expert support.

There are a couple of other great platforms that address specific aspects of mental health.

- **Calm:** An app for meditation and sleep.
- **Replika:** An AI chatbot that builds a digital persona of the user based on personality features, eventually helping them to cope with stress while improving their mental health.

By embracing technology and data-driven approaches while fostering a culture of empathy and openness, organizations can create a more holistic and personalized approach to mental well-being. Platforms like Woebot and Wysa showcase the potential of advancements in mental health management, paving the way for a brighter and more inclusive future of mental health support in the workplace.

Mind-Body Sync: Charting Mental Wellness Like Physical Fitness

The future of mental health management lies in recognizing the intricate link between psychological and physiological factors. As we acknowledge the mind-body connection, we gain a deeper understanding of how physical health can significantly influence psychological well-being. Integrating data from both domains empowers individuals to have a comprehensive view of their overall well-being, fostering proactive and personalized approaches to both physical and mental health care.

Wearable technology has revolutionized how we track and manage our physical health, and its potential in monitoring mental health is equally promising. These devices can track biometric indicators of stress, such as heart rate variability and skin conductance, providing insights into an individual's emotional state. By wearing these unobtrusive devices, individuals gain real-time feedback on their mental state, empowering them to recognize and manage stress more effectively.

Apple Watch's OS 10 introduces a groundbreaking Mindfulness app, emphasizing the company's commitment to mental well-being. This app encourages users to cultivate mindfulness and emotional awareness through guided meditations and breathing exercises. Users can discreetly log their momentary emotions and daily moods, creating a valuable resource for self-reflection and understanding. Moreover, the Mindfulness app seamlessly integrates with other health and well-being features, providing users with a holistic approach to managing their overall health.

Oura rings, along with monitoring sleep and other biometrics, sense changes in the body associated with stress. The wearable device then adjusts the user's daily goals and gives feedback.

Looking ahead, the convergence of psychological and physiological data doesn't need to be only through wearable technology. Virtual AI employee assistants should be able to gather physiological data from the employee's wearable and leverage the data to come up with personalized plans to manage the work challenges. The future of mental health tracking is one where individuals are empowered to take charge of their mental wellness, fostering a balanced and thriving approach to overall health and happiness.

Bridging the Mental Health Divide: Overcoming Support Hurdles

As we envision the future of mental health support, it is crucial to address the pressing challenges that hinder individuals from accessing timely and adequate professional care.

Many individuals, especially in remote areas, face geographical barriers that limit their access to mental health professionals. Continuing to leverage telehealth and digital platforms to bridge these gaps enables employees to access mental health support conveniently and inclusively.

The increasing demand for mental health services has put a strain on mental health professionals, leading to clinician shortages and burnout. To sustain a resilient mentally healthy workforce, it is crucial to implement supportive measures that prioritize clinician well-being. Integration of technology and AI in self-care, initial assessments, and post-care follow-ups can augment clinician capacity, alleviating their workload and improving overall service quality.

Long waiting times for psychologist consultations can deter individuals from seeking timely help. By identifying bottlenecks in the consultation process, organizations can streamline intake and assessment procedures, reducing waiting times and ensuring faster access to care. Virtual AI assistants can play a vital role in providing immediate support and mental health first aid to those facing acute challenges, enabling individuals to receive timely assistance before their scheduled consultation.

In the quest for improved mental health support, addressing these challenges is crucial to creating a future where mental well-being is accessible, efficient, and proactive. By embracing innovative solutions, leveraging technology, and prioritizing the well-being of mental health professionals, we can forge a path towards a more resilient and inclusive mental health support system.

On-the-Spot Sanity: First Aid for Mental Health at Work

Day-to-day work challenges can have a cumulative effect on an individual's mental health. It is essential for the future of mental health support to prioritize immediate assistance for employees facing these challenges. By offering timely support, organizations can intervene early, preventing minor stressors from escalating into more significant mental health issues. Through this proactive approach, employees are equipped with coping mechanisms and resilience to navigate work challenges with greater ease and mental fortitude.

As mental health first aid gains prominence, organizations must integrate it into their workplace strategies. Training employees in mental health first aid and strongly encouraging them to use it equips them with the skills and knowledge to recognize and respond to mental health challenges among their colleagues.

In conclusion, immediate mental health first aid is a crucial aspect of the future of mental health support in the workplace. By distinguishing between different stressors, providing timely assistance, and integrating mental health first aid into workplace strategies, organizations can build a resilient and mentally healthy workforce. As we proceed, investing in these proactive approaches will undoubtedly contribute to a more compassionate, supportive, and thriving work environment.

AI vs. Therapists: A Perspective

The latest debate surrounding AI assistants replacing mental health therapists or psychologists has sparked significant interest and controversy in the field of mental health care. While I see significant advantages in leveraging AI assistants to help employees manage their challenges and boost their mental health, it is all about striking a balance between understanding how much AI can augment mental health professional capacity, where exactly it can complement a therapist, and where human intervention is absolutely required in addition to ethical considerations and data privacy.

Some of the key advantages of AI assistants are listed below.

- **Non-Judgmental:** People seeking mental health support often struggle with opening up due to the fear of being judged by another human being. AI assistants, being devoid of emotions and biases, provide a non-judgmental and safe environment for individuals to express their thoughts and emotions freely.
- **All-time availability:** AI assistants can offer 24x7 assistance, which is a crucial advantage in addressing mental health

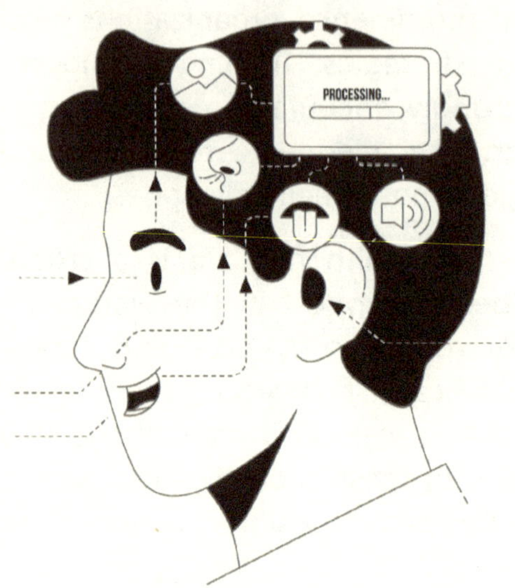

crises. Traditional therapists have limited availability, making it challenging for patients to access immediate support during emergencies. AI assistants, on the other hand, can ensure continuous assistance and guidance to those in need.

- **Scalability:** With the increase in mental health challenges and the limited availability of mental health professionals, AI assistants can help scale up the support on a global scale.
- **Consistent quality:** Human therapists may vary in their approach, expertise, and personal biases, which can affect the treatment experience for different individuals. In contrast, AI assistants are designed to adhere to a standardized and evidence-based approach, providing consistent support and guidance to all users. They can leverage vast databases of clinical research and best practices, ensuring that users receive reliable and up-to-date information and interventions. This consistency in service quality can enhance the overall effectiveness and reliability of mental health support.
- **Geographical availability:** Currently employees working in some remote locations do not have access to highly qualified mental health professionals. This can be easily addressed by AI assistants.
- **Leveraging data**: The ability to collect and analyze data from numerous interactions enables AI assistants to continuously learn and improve their responses, potentially making them more effective over time.

- **Augmenting capacity:** AI assistants have the potential to significantly augment the capacity of mental health practitioners by assisting in various stages of the therapeutic process. Firstly, they can conduct initial assessments and screenings, gathering essential information about a patient's mental health status and history. This enables mental health professionals to save time and focus on deeper therapeutic interventions rather than spending it on routine data collection.

- **Mental first aid:** AI assistants can provide immediate first aid and crisis support, which is especially valuable in situations where individuals require urgent assistance. They can recognize signs of distress and provide appropriate coping strategies or recommend seeking professional help promptly.

- **Post-care follow-ups:** AI assistants can play a vital role in post-care follow-ups. After sessions with mental health professionals, they can reach out to patients, monitor their progress, and offer personalized resources and exercises to reinforce therapeutic insights and skills learned during therapy. This continuous support can help patients maintain momentum in their healing journey and improve treatment outcomes.

- **Progress Tracking:** With the ability to gather data, AI assistants are able to track and evaluate the progress and accordingly provide timely feedback and support. When users are making noticeable progress towards their goals, AI assistants can offer positive reinforcement and encouragement. On the other hand, if users are not making sufficient progress or are deviating from their desired path, AI assistants can offer corrective actions and suggestions. These interventions can be based on analyzing patterns in the data and identifying potential obstacles that might be hindering progress. By offering tailored advice and strategies, AI assistants help users recalibrate their efforts and stay on track.

- **On-going Maintenance**: AI assistants play a crucial role in supporting on-going mental health maintenance by providing continuous attention. Furthermore, AI can adapt its strategies based on user feedback and changing circumstances. For example, if a user reports feeling particularly stressed, the AI can adjust its recommendations and interactions to address that specific concern. Over time, the AI can track patterns in the user's mood and behavior, offering insights and suggestions to proactively manage potential mental health challenges.

In summary, if used appropriately, AI assistants can help significantly in leading more effective and personalized mental health care overall.

Whole-Person Wellness: Beyond the Basics in Employee Care

To create a future-ready approach to employee well-being, organizations must integrate both mental and physical health initiatives. By offering holistic well-being programs that encompass physical exercise, nutrition, and mental health awareness, organizations can support employees' overall health and resilience. Moreover, promoting work-life balance and flexibility allows employees to maintain a healthy harmony between their personal and professional lives. Fostering a culture of preventive mental health support empowers employees to address potential challenges proactively, ensuring a mentally healthy and engaged workforce.

In the future, organizations will recognize the critical role of employee engagement in mental health management. Engaged employees are more likely to experience higher levels of job satisfaction, which positively influences their mental well-being. By creating meaningful and fulfilling work experiences, organizations can foster a sense of purpose and belonging among employees, contributing to their overall mental health and happiness.

Recognizing the direct correlation between employee engagement and productivity, organizations will prioritize mental health initiatives that enhance engagement levels, resulting in a more productive and successful workforce.

The future of employee well-being will be characterized by the seamless integration of employee assistance and collaboration tools. Technology-enabled platforms can provide accessible and confidential mental health support to employees, promoting early interventions and timely assistance. These platforms will offer a wide range of resources, including mental health professionals, self-help tools, and coping strategies. Moreover, these tools will facilitate collaboration among employees, allowing for peer support, sharing of experiences, and collective learning, which further strengthens the sense of community and support within the organization.

State of Mind: The Government's Role in Championing Mental Health

Governments worldwide are acknowledging the importance of mental health as a critical public health priority. In the future, we can expect governments to allocate more resources and funding to build robust mental health infrastructure. This includes expanding mental health services, promoting mental health education, and investing in research to address emerging challenges. Governments will also forge partnerships with the private sector to create comprehensive support systems that encompass workplaces, communities, and educational institutions, fostering a holistic approach to mental health management.

Governments will enact legislative measures to promote mental health in organizations. In the future, we can anticipate stricter regulations that compel employers to prioritize mental health in the workplace. This may include guidelines for managing workplace stress, promoting work-life balance, and addressing mental health issues proactively. Governments will also mandate employers to implement mental health programs, such as employee assistance programs (EAPs), to ensure access to support and resources for employees. Additionally, governments may provide incentives to employers who actively invest in proactive well-being initiatives, fostering a culture of mental health and employee well-being.

In conclusion, the future of mental health support in the global work landscape holds great promise, fueled by forward-looking initiatives and policies. As organizations embrace a proactive and holistic approach to employee well-being, mental health will become a priority woven into the fabric of workplace culture. By recognizing the importance of mental wellness, providing immediate support for day-to-day work challenges, and integrating mental health first aid into strategies, organizations can foster a resilient and thriving workforce.

The integration of technology and AI-powered platforms unlocks new possibilities in mental health support, enabling remote consultations, real-time assessments and advice, personalized well-being plans, and post-care follow-ups. Wearable technology paves the way for monitoring mental health akin to physical health, potentially feeding the data back to virtual AI assistants at the workplace, empowering individuals to maintain and boost their mental health.

The global landscape also showcases progressive case studies of countries implementing forward-looking policies. These examples inspire further action, creating a ripple effect of positive change that prioritizes mental health management in organizations.

With a collective commitment to mental health and well-being, we envision a future where mental health support is seamless, inclusive, and preventive. By nurturing a culture of empathy, support, and openness, organizations will pave the way for a workforce that thrives not only professionally but also personally.

Chapter Summary

The future of the global work landscape emphasizes mental wellness as a crucial aspect of employee performance and well-being.

- Organizations must embrace platforms that offer proactive mental well-being support, real-time advice, and engagement to create resilient workplaces worldwide.
- Innovative technology, such as virtual AI assistants and wearable devices, enables the tracking of mental health, similar to physical health, promoting holistic well-being.
- Existing standard wellness platforms and EAPs have limitations, necessitating the exploration of newer solutions for comprehensive mental health support.
- Government policies worldwide are favoring mental health management, with legislative measures and case studies showcasing progressive initiatives.
- Immediate mental health first aid is vital to address day-to-day work challenges and foster employee resilience and coping mechanisms.
- A holistic approach to employee well-being blends mental and physical health initiatives, emphasizing work-life balance and preventive mental health support.
- Employee engagement plays a crucial role in mental health management, influencing productivity and overall well-being in the workplace.
- Utilizing employee assistance and collaboration tools empowers organizations to provide immediate support and foster a culture of psychological safety.
- By prioritizing mental health, organizations can create a supportive and compassionate work culture, leading to a thriving and resilient workforce ready to face future challenges.

Author Bio

Roopa Raj is an esteemed thought leader in the realm of technology, celebrated for her profound technical expertise, leadership, and global impact. With an extensive career marked by innovation and insight, Roopa brings a wealth of experience to the intersection of the evolving technology landscape and workforce dynamics.

As a distinguished figure with a rich history of navigating global roles and guiding leading enterprises towards rapid and sustainable growth, Roopa's journey encompasses a profound understanding of the challenges and opportunities posed by digital transformations. Her insights into the silent struggles of employees across the world offer a unique perspective on the evolving landscape of the modern workplace and its impact on mental health.

Having embraced leadership positions across varied domains and regions, Roopa possesses an unparalleled understanding of the intricacies of multi-geography and multicultural team dynamics. Her vision and accomplishments have transcended specific workplaces, leaving an indelible mark on the broader industry.

Roopa's ethos centers around fostering high-performing cultures that empower organizations to attract, nurture, and retain top talent. A firm advocate for diversity and inclusion, she champions the cause of equity in the workforce, inspiring change by example.

Beyond her corporate endeavors, Roopa's commitment extends to mentoring deep-tech start-ups. Her expertise extends naturally to the written word, as she addresses workplace challenges and provides insights on how technological advancements, specifically AI/ML, can help in predictive and preventive mental well-being across enterprises.

In this book, Roopa delves into the complexities of the modern workplace, emphasizing the significance of mental health and its synergy with evolving work cultures. Through her insightful narratives and forward-looking perspectives, she shapes a compelling vision for a future where innovation thrives, diverse voices are heard, and holistic well-being takes center stage. Roopa Raj's authorship embodies a journey of leadership, understanding, and advocacy that resonates across industries and borders.

www.ingramcontent.com/pod-product-compliance
Lightning Source LLC
LaVergne TN
LVHW041035150826
845672LV00001B/327

* 9 7 9 8 8 9 0 6 7 8 5 8 4 *